GUIDE TO
PLANNING YOUR
FINANCIAL FUTURE

THE EASY-TO-READ GUIDE TO PLANNING FOR

RETIREMENT

KENNETH M. MORRIS
VIRGINIA B. MORRIS

LIGHTBULB
PRESS

LIGHTBULB PRESS
Project Team

Design Director Dave Wilder
Design Assistant Katharina Menner
Editors Mavis Morris, Tania Sanchez
Production Thomas F. Trojan
Illustration Krista K. Glasser, Barnes Tilney
Photography Andy Shen

SPECIAL THANKS
Hugh Joyner and John A. Gill
Robert Berger, Carla Fey and Richard Irving
Gregory Hess
Ira Cohen

PICTURE CREDITS
The Bettmann Archive, New York (pages 24, 68, 69, 70)
Comstock, New York (pages 40, 58, 59, 60, 82, 84)
FPG, New York (pages 36, 40, 60, 61, 83, 84)
General Motors Corporation (page 95)
The Image Bank, New York (pages 42, 54, 55, 61, 71, 84)
Reuters/Bettmann, New York (page 71)
UPI/Bettmann, New York (pages 61, 68, 70, 71)

LIGHTBULB
PRESS ®

*I*n a world where everything seems to be changing, doing all you can to build a secure financial future presents new and sometimes daunting challenges.

More than ever, the investments and financial planning decisions you make while you are still working will affect the income you have after you retire and the financial security of those who survive you.

But making the right decisions isn't easy, even though your financial future is at stake:

What happens to your retirement assets if you change jobs? And how do you manage optional and required withdrawals from tax-deferred plans?

If you qualify to make catch-up contributions to these plans, is that a smart use of your investment dollars?

How can you pass along the wealth you've accumulated to the people that arc important to you?

Who will pay for the healthcare you may need as you get older?

This *Guide* tackles these and equally pressing questions. It explores the often perplexing relationship between Social Security, pensions, and self-directed retirement savings. It describes a variety of ways to create a long-term stream of retirement income. It explains minimum required withdrawals from retirement plans. And it summarizes the ways in which estate and gift tax laws are scheduled to change in the years ahead—and how those changes may affect your financial decisions.

Despite the uncertainties that we all face, and the changes that are sure to come, we were yet again convinced, in preparing this edition, that having the information and the confidence you need to make the best choices is key to a sound financial future.

Kenneth M. Morris
Virginia B. Morris

GUIDE TO PLANNING YOUR FINANCIAL FUTURE

CONTENTS

The Retirement Marathon

Planning your financial future is planning for retirement—
and having the money to enjoy it.

In 1900, retirement wasn't a hot topic. Most employers didn't offer pensions, there was no Social Security, and the average life expectancy was 50.

But more than a century later, everything's changed. More than a million people retire every year, many in their early 60s—and they expect to live into their 80s or longer. Current estimates suggest that a million or more people now in their 40s can expect to live to be 100 or more.

READY, SET, GO
The general wisdom is that planning your financial future starts with your first job. That's when you can begin putting money into an individual retirement account (IRA). Even though you'll probably have lots of shorter-term reasons to invest, such as buying a car or a home, you should be thinking early on about long-term goals: your financial security and the security of those you care about. You'll quickly discover that there are lots of ways to invest for the future—including some that have built-in tax advantages.

In Your 20s: Getting Started

You can get a head start on building your financial future if you start early. The two opportunities you don't want to pass up:

- Contributing to a **voluntary tax-deferred retirement plan**

- Setting up an **investment account** with a mutual fund, brokerage, or bank

While you may be paying off college debts or struggling to meet living expenses, the advantages of getting an early start on a long-term investment plan are too good to pass up.

Ideally, you should be investing up to 10% of your pretax income. If you're in an employer sponsored retirement plan that deducts your contribution from your salary, your taxable income will be reduced. That means tax savings—a reward for doing the right thing.

Though some of what you've put aside should be **liquid**, or easy to turn into cash, the best investments are generally stocks or stock mutual funds. The growth they provide usually justifies the risk of possible setbacks in the short term.

In Your 30s & 40s: Hitting Your Stride

Even while you're juggling your income to pay for things that might seem more pressing, like buying a home, supporting a family, or anticipating your children's college expenses, you need to build your long-term investments.

One technique is to split the amount you invest between long- and short-term goals. Even if you put less into long-term plans than you'd like, these investments have the potential to grow, especially if you're building on a portfolio you started in your 20s. Experts agree that long-term investments should still be in stocks or stock mutual funds, but short-term investments should be more liquid.

Keep in mind that investing for the long term is good for your current financial situation too:

- **You save on taxes by participating in a salary reduction plan**

- **You may qualify for a mortgage more easily if you have investment assets**

- **You can borrow from some retirement investments without incurring taxes and penalties**

WHAT THE FUTURE HOLDS

The truth is that retirement age is relative, not fixed. Many government workers retire after 20 years of service—sometimes as soon as their early 40s. Some people work productively through their 80s, thinking of retirement as something other people do. Many others retire the first day they're eligible. Still others leave work unwillingly, taking early retirement packages they can't refuse.

What you do about retirement may fit one of those patterns, or maybe one you design for yourself. But whether retirement is a long way off, or sneaking up on you faster than you care to imagine, planning for your financial future has three main ingredients:

- **Your financial security**
- **Adequate healthcare**
- **Benefits for your heirs**

In Your 40s & 50s: The Far Turn

You may be earning more than before, but you may be spending more too. College expenses can wreak havoc on long-term investment goals. So can expensive hobbies or moving to a bigger house.

On the other hand, if you've established good investing habits—like participating in a salary reduction plan and putting money into stocks and stock mutual funds—your long-term goals should be on track. You may also find that the demands on your current income eventually begin to decrease: the mortgage gets paid off, the children eventually grow up, or you inherit assets from your parents.

That means you can begin to put more money into your long-term portfolio—through your employer's voluntary salary reduction plans, through mutual fund or brokerage accounts, and through some income-producing investments such as CDs and bonds.

In Your 60s: The Home Stretch

When you start thinking seriously about retirement, you have to be sure you have enough money to live comfortably. If you have income coming in from a pension and investments, you'll have the flexibility to retire when you want.

Because many people can expect to live 20 or 30 years after they retire, you'll want to continue to invest even as you begin collecting on your retirement plans. One approach is to deposit earnings from certain investments into an account earmarked to make new ones. Another is to time the maturity dates of bonds or certificates of deposit (CD), so that you have capital to reinvest if a good opportunity comes along.

Some of the other financial decisions you'll be facing may be dictated by government rules about when and what you must withdraw from your retirement accounts. Others may be driven by your concerns about healthcare or your desire to leave money to your heirs. At the least, you'll have to consider:

- **Shifting investments to produce more income with fewer risks, in case of a sudden downturn in the financial markets**

- **Rolling over retirement payouts to preserve their tax-deferred status**

- **Setting up an estate plan that will distribute your assets as you wish**

AN EASY FORMULA
One conservative rule of thumb for deciding what investments to make: Add a percent sign to your age. Then put no more than that percentage of your money in fixed income investments like bonds or CDs. The rest goes into stocks.

Planning for the Future

To live comfortably after you retire, you have to be realistic about how much you'll need to pay the bills.

Good health is wonderful. So is a nice place to live. But what you really need when you retire is money—money to pay your bills, with enough left over to do the things you want. The general rule of thumb is this: You'll need 70% to 80% of what you're spending before you retire, more if you have expensive hobbies or plan to travel extensively. For example,

CURRENT INCOME X **80%** = **PROJECTED NEED**

if your gross income while you're working is $6,000 a month—that's $72,000 a year—you'll probably need $4,800 a month, or about $57,600 a year, after you retire.

UP OR DOWN?

You can be pretty sure some of your living expenses will shrink after you retire, but others are equally certain to go up. Planning your financial future includes anticipating those changes.

WHAT COSTS LESS

- By the time you retire, you'll probably have paid off your mortgage.

- Unless you were older than average when your children were born, you will have finished paying for their educations.

- If you commuted to work, you'll probably spend less on day-to-day travel and restaurant meals. You may need only one car, and will probably spend less on clothes and make fewer visits to the dry cleaner.

WHAT COSTS MORE

- Home maintenance costs and property taxes tend to go up, not down, over time, unless you move to a smaller place or to a state with lower taxes.

- If you're home all the time, your utility bills may increase.

- Home and car insurance are apt to increase.

- Medical expenses, including the cost of insurance, often increase significantly over preretirement costs. These costs will continue to rise as employers cut back on healthcare coverage in general, and for retirees in particular. One of the major expenses you may face, and one of the most controversial insurance issues, is paying for prescription drugs.

INFLATION'S BITE

Inflation is another factor you have to consider when planning your retirement budget. If you were retiring this June, for example, you'd need 80% of what you were spending in May. But next June you'd need more money to pay for the same goods and services.

That's because of **inflation**, the gradual increase in the cost of living. Inflation has averaged 3% annually since 1926, hovering around that point since the early 1990s. It has sometimes been much higher though, hitting 13.5% in 1980 and averaging 6% through the 1980s.

That means if you're planning on a 20-year retirement, you'll need more than double the income in the 20th year than you do in the first, just to stay even. How can you manage that, especially if you're not working any more? The surest way is by earning money on your investments, at a rate that tops the rate of inflation.

DOING THE MATH

While it might take a long time to estimate your retirement needs if you were doing the math yourself, you can use one of the software programs often called retirement planning calculators available on financial services websites or on CD-ROMs. Some of these programs—and a number of the websites—have been developed primarily to provide an independent planning resource. Others are sponsored by mutual fund companies or brokerage firms to offer planning that incorporates an introduction to their own products and services.

The software programs are generally easy to use. All you have to do is plug in the financial information they ask for, along with details about your plans for the future. The program will project how much more you'll need to invest to have enough money to retire on.

Or, you might prefer to work with a financial adviser or planner to identify investment strategies you can use to help meet your retirement goals within the timeframe you set.

A MATTER OF TIMING

If you start investing when you begin working—perhaps 35 years or more before you plan to retire—and you put away 10% of what you earn each year, you should have a head start on your long-term financial security. If you can average an 8% annual growth rate on your investments, and ride out the inevitable ups and downs in the markets over the years, once you turn 65 you should be able to replace a substantial percentage of what you were earning before you retired.

The longer you wait to begin investing, the greater the challenge you face in accumulating the assets you need. While that could happen—say if a period of strong growth kicked in just as you got started—you can't count on it. And the fewer years your investment assets have to compound, the harder they can be hit by a market downturn.

For each year you delay, you'll have to put aside a larger percentage of your annual earnings to build the same level of reserves as someone who began at an earlier age. And chances are you'll have a hard time finding that much money to invest, no matter how important you know it is to save.

THERE AREN'T ANY SCHOLARSHIPS

In some ways, investing for retirement is like investing for college. When you start, these goals seem a long way in the future—though they sneak up on you more quickly than you ever imagine.

The big difference is that there are no scholarships for retirement, and no loans either. True, you may have a pension, and most people can expect income from Social Security. And you can go on working longer than you may have planned. But the factor that separates just getting by after you retire from living the life you were looking forward to usually comes down to the investments you make while you are working.

SPECIAL CASES

You may have certain special advantages in planning your financial future. Veterans, for example, can apply for mortgages, healthcare coverage, and disability benefits through the Veterans Administration (VA). They may also qualify for local tax breaks and get pension credit for their years on active service.

Union members and members of professional and other organizations may qualify for health and life insurance at lower rates than those available to the general population, or for other kinds of reduced-rate goods and services. Sometimes members of the clergy are offered discounts too.

In any case, you should check with any groups you're part of for the long-term financial advantages that may come with your membership. The larger ones may also keep you up to date on tax and other changes that affect your finances directly, through newsletters, journals, or other publications.

Protecting Your Future

The best protection for a comfortable future is a strong financial plan.

To safeguard your own financial future and the future of people who matter to you, you need a strategy that builds your assets at the same time that it protects them against the assaults of taxes, inflation, and the general costs of living.

Job-related pensions and retirement savings plans, plus the investments you make throughout your working life, are the basic asset-building materials you need. The sooner you begin hammering them into place, the stronger a position you can build. By writing a will and perhaps creating a trust or two, you can go on protecting the security you've built for your heirs to enjoy.

THREATS TO YOUR FINANCIAL SECURITY

INFLATION
Inflation erodes your buying power as prices go up. Your income may not keep pace.

HEALTHCARE
The cost of healthcare has been increasing much faster than inflation in general.

ESTATE TAXES
Estate taxes may reduce what you've accumulated to leave to your heirs.

WITHDRAWAL PENALTIES
You have to pay a penalty if you take too little from your traditional IRA after you turn 70½.

INCOME TAXES
Income taxes can be your single largest expense, even after you retire.

LOCAL TAXES
Some places are much more expensive to live in because they have higher taxes.

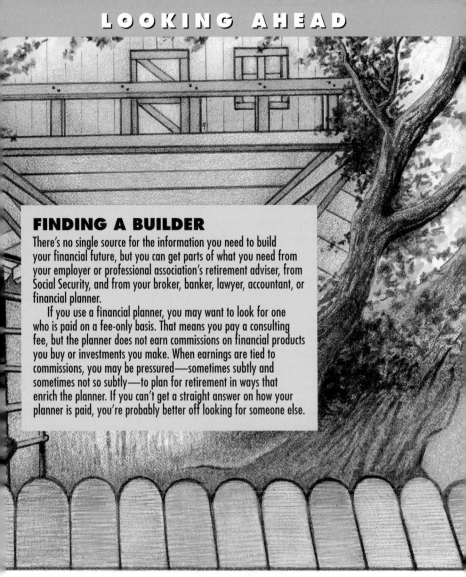

FINDING A BUILDER

There's no single source for the information you need to build your financial future, but you can get parts of what you need from your employer or professional association's retirement adviser, from Social Security, and from your broker, banker, lawyer, accountant, or financial planner.

If you use a financial planner, you may want to look for one who is paid on a fee-only basis. That means you pay a consulting fee, but the planner does not earn commissions on financial products you buy or investments you make. When earnings are tied to commissions, you may be pressured—sometimes subtly and sometimes not so subtly—to plan for retirement in ways that enrich the planner. If you can't get a straight answer on how your planner is paid, you're probably better off looking for someone else.

THE MAIN PROTECTIONS

EMPLOYER PENSIONS
Pensions can provide a significant part of your post-retirement income.

RETIREMENT SAVINGS PLANS
You can take advantage of tax-deferred or tax-free investing opportunities.

SOCIAL SECURITY
By contributing while you work, you earn the right to income after you retire.

WISE INVESTMENTS
The difference between just getting by and living comfortably will probably depend on your investments.

MEDICARE
You'll be entitled to basic medical coverage after you retire if you contribute while you work.

HEALTH INSURANCE
You can buy health insurance to help ward off financial catastrophe.

WILLS AND TRUSTS
With advance planning, you can reduce estate taxes and benefit your heirs.

Money Matters

Taking care of business won't take any less time after you retire, though you may save money.

If you think of retirement as a simpler time of life, you may be in for a shock, at least in the paperwork department. That's because things your employer handled—tax withholding and health insurance payments, for example—are now your personal responsibility.

On top of that, you'll probably have to spend more time moving money among accounts to maintain your cash flow once you get your final paycheck. And if you're taking money out of tax-deferred retirement plans, you'll have to be on top of the withdrawal rules. They're different for different accounts.

There's also the added time and expense of making photocopies of medical bills for your records. You'll need them as backup if you want to contest a Medicare decision or claim a tax deduction. But if being retired won't save you time, it may save you some money on different types of taxes.

TAX MATTERS

One of the biggest changes after retirement may be paying estimated income taxes four times a year. Of course, if you've worked for yourself or had a lot of non-salary income, filling out the forms and writing a check to the IRS (and your state tax department) is nothing new. But if you've always had your income taxes withheld from your salary, figuring out what you owe each quarter can be an eye-opener.

You make your first payment on April 15—the same day the previous year's tax return is due—and the others on June 15, September 15, and the following January 15. You use Form 1040-ES, "Estimated Tax for Individuals", to figure and pay what you owe. In most cases, you must prepay most of your total tax bill, though the required percentage may change from year to year.

12

Long-Term Care
Insurance Application

How to Complete this Application

1) Each person applying for cov...

MEDICAL MATTERS

Your doctor's office may file your Medicare claim forms and coordinate with your supplemental insurance provider. But it's important to keep accurate records in case you want to appeal a denial of coverage. You may also be able to deduct a percentage of your costs on your tax return if you have large out-of-pocket expenses.

Nondeductible IRAs
(Contributions, Distributions, and Basis)
► Please see What Records Must I Keep? below.
► Attach to Form 1040, Form 1040A, or Form 1040NR.

INVESTMENT MATTERS

After you retire, you'll probably depend on your investments to supply part—perhaps a large part—of your living expenses. That might mean shifting some of your portfolio from growth to income, and deciding how much you can spend each year without outliving your assets. After you reach 70½, you'll also have to start regular withdrawals from your traditional IRAs and from your qualified retirement plans if you're already retired. You'll also have to pay the income taxes you've deferred as you withdraw from these accounts.

THE SMALLER TAX BITE

Once you retire or reach the age of 65, or both, your tax picture often changes—usually for the better. After you stop working, you won't have Social Security taxes withheld. Pensions are reported on a Form 1099R, not on a W2 form.

While you'll still owe federal income taxes after you retire, chances are you may pay less than you did while you were working, especially if your total income is reduced. That's because once you turn 65 you may be able to take advantage of several provisions in the tax law that lower your bill, even though the tax rates themselves aren't influenced by your age.

In the first place, you can take a larger standard deduction than a younger person can, and you can take an even larger deduction if both you and your spouse are over 65. And you can make slightly more money than a younger person before you must file a return at all unless you have self-employment income.

You may also be eligible for a tax credit, which you can subtract directly from the tax that's due if your income falls below a specific amount. IRS Publication 524, "Credit for the Elderly or the Disabled," provides the information and worksheets you need to figure out where you stand.

Department of the Treasury
Internal Revenue Service

Publication 524
Cat. No. 150485

Credit for the Elderly or the Disabled

For use in preparing
Returns

OTHER TAX BREAKS

You may not owe tax on your Social Security benefit if your total income (including half your Social Security) is less than $25,000 if you're single, or $32,000 if you're married. If your income is more than that, though, you may owe tax on 50% to 85% of your benefit. On the brighter side, the state where you live may not tax your pension—or you may consider moving to a state that doesn't. The rules are different in each state, so you'll have to check. But states can't tax pension money you earned within their borders if you've changed your legal residence to another state. For example, if you worked in New York, but now live in Florida, you don't owe New York income tax on the pension you receive from your former employer.

Making Critical Choices

You'll have the answers you need down the road if you ask the right questions now.

The idea of retiring isn't new. People who grew too old or too ill stopped working and stayed home long before pensions and Social Security. But as people stop working sooner and live longer, the retirement experience takes on a different meaning. Not only can you expect more years of retirement than of adolescence, but they can be a lot more satisfying and rewarding.

Q: What financial decisions do I make?

A: Set your retirement timeline

55
- You can usually begin withdrawing from 401(k)s, 403(b)s, and certain other plans without a 10% penalty if you retire, quit or are fired.

You may be eligible for full pension benefits from some employer plans if you have enough years of service.

59½
- You can withdraw money from tax-deferred savings plans (IRAs, Keoghs, SEPs) without paying a 10% penalty.

60
- You can receive Social Security benefits if you are a widow or widower.

SOME CRITICAL CHOICES

As morbid as it sounds, even as you're looking forward to retirement, you need to deal with two critical issues: the medical decisions you want made if you're ill, and what you want to happen to your property after you die. If you don't make your intentions clear, your family and friends face a greater emotional burden and often greater expense than they might otherwise. And you might not approve of the decisions that are made without your direction.

It's not enough just to tell people what you want to happen. State laws often require written proof of your wishes concerning life-prolonging treatment if you're critically ill, just as they require a legal will to transfer your property.

Q: How do I make my healthcare wishes known?

A: A Living Will

A **living will** is a document that describes the kind of medical treatment you want—and don't want—if you are terminally ill or in a permanent vegetative state (which means you're unconscious, not able to communicate, and unlikely to get better). In writing your living will, you should be as specific as possible about the kinds of drugs and medical procedures you have in mind and the situations under which they should—or should not be—used.

Though almost all states accept living wills, the laws of each state are a little different, so you want to be sure that the living will you

Q: How can someone make decisions for me?

A: Healthcare Proxy

A living will makes your healthcare wishes known, but it does not always guarantee they will be followed. Someone will still have to authorize treatment, or make a decision not to continue it. You can appoint a healthcare agent or surrogate in a signed and witnessed document known as a **healthcare proxy,** or you can grant a **durable power of attorney for healthcare** to someone who will make the decisions you would have wanted.

You should be sure to ask permission of the person you name and describe your feelings about your care in detail. Without understanding what you want, it would be very difficult for your surrogate to see that your wishes are carried out. Because there are still unresolved legal questions about the extent of a surrogate's authority, it probably makes sense to get legal advice in preparing these documents.

62

- You may be eligible for full pension benefits from your employer.
- You can receive reduced Social Security benefits.

65

- You can receive full pension benefits from most employers.
- You can get full Social Security benefits if you were born before 1943.
- You qualify for Medicare benefits.

70

- You should begin to collect your Social Security benefits if you haven't already, because your base benefit has reached its maximum.

70½

- You must begin withdrawals from your traditional IRAs, but not from Roth IRAs or from employer sponsored retirement plans if you're still working.

sign meets local requirements. One area that can cause conflict, for example, is whether a hospital will respect your wish not to receive food and water. Some states require that feeding be continued as long as you are alive. Many allow it to be ended if that's what you've indicated in your living will.

Since professional caregivers generally choose to prolong life when possible, you probably don't need a living will if you agree with that approach. But if you're opposed to extraordinary measures to keep you alive, such as heart-lung machines, intravenous feeding, and similar techniques, you should sign a living will and ask two people to witness it. You should also be sure your family and your doctor know that you've signed a living will and where they can find a copy.

You don't need a lawyer to draw up the document, although if you're in the process of preparing a regular will, you can sign both at once, probably for little or no additional charge. Or, you can get information from Partnership for Caring at 202-296-8071 or by visiting their website at www.partnershipforcaring.org.

THE RIGHT TIME

When's the right time to sign a living will and a healthcare proxy? If you have strong feelings about the way you want to be cared for if you're ill or injured, you can do it as soon as you reach the age of majority in the state where you live, either 18 or 21. It's easy to think of healthcare as a problem for the elderly, but the truth is most of the major court cases involving a patient's right to receive a particular type of treatment or her right to die have dealt with young people—often in their late teens or early 20s—who were injured in an accident or became ill unexpectedly.

DRAFTING A WILL

If you want your wishes about the transfer of your property and the care of your dependent children carried out after you die, you must **execute**, or sign, an official will and have it witnessed. Young people, and those without dependents or property, may be able to postpone making a will. But anyone else is making a serious mistake by putting it off.

Where to Live?

Is your home your castle, or just a place to hang your hat?

Where will you live when you retire? The majority of older Americans stay put, not only in the same community where they've spent their working lives, but often in the same house or apartment where they've been living. Of those who do move, 81% settle within the same state. Only about 19% actually move out of state.

One increasingly popular option, if you can swing it financially, is **sojourning**, or using your primary residence as home base, but shifting to a second home during part of the year. People who enjoy the flexibility and change of scene consider it an ideal way to enjoy the best of two worlds. For others, who've tried but abandoned it, it's rootless and unsettling.

WHICH HOME SWEET HOME

MARKET FORCES

If you own your home outright or have only a small mortgage, you can probably make enough from selling your home to move wherever you want, especially if you're in the market for a smaller place. In fact, most people sell their homes for more than they paid for them unless their neighborhood has gone downhill or the property itself needs a lot of work.

Remember, though, that real estate isn't a liquid investment, and you can't count on how much the property will be worth when you're ready to sell. The housing market is sometimes slow, or depressed, which might mean you can't sell at all or have to settle for a lower price than you counted on. The reverse is also true: If real estate is in a boom period, you'll make more on your house than you expected. But you might also have to pay more for the place you want to move to.

LIVING ABROAD

Every month, Social Security sends almost 400,000 checks to to beneficiaries, not all of them U.S. citizens, living outside the country. And that doesn't include the people who have their checks deposited in banks at home. There are lots of financial advantages, and probably an equal number of drawbacks, to making the move abroad. Most of them hinge on tax issues, though currency fluctuation, healthcare, and estate planning are also involved.

SHARING YOUR SPACE

If the cost or the work involved in keeping up your home is a problem, one option is to share your living space, either with friends or family members who split the costs, or with tenants who pay rent.

Having people in the house can be a real plus, since they provide companionship as well as help with finances or household chores. There's certainly a tradition behind it. But, before you commit yourself to sharing, you'll want to consider the arrangements carefully, and check restrictions in local zoning laws.

WEIGHING THE FACTORS

You can weigh financial and other factors to help you decide whether to move or to stay put. They include:

- Annual cost of maintenance and upkeep, including mortgage, utilities, and taxes
- Physical demands of maintenance and upkeep
- General cost of living, including food, transportation, and entertainment
- Availability of quality healthcare
- Distance from family and friends

member because you don't want to risk having the transfer considered a taxable gift.

The new owner pays off the cost of the home over the term of the agreement, and you pay rent out of the income you're collecting on the sale. To prevent a problem if you want to continue living in your home when the agreement ends, you can buy an annuity to replace the income you'll need to pay the rent.

There are often estate-planning advantages in sale-leasebacks. If you sell to a relative or close friend, you can avoid probate and potentially reduce their inheritance taxes.

SELL BUT STAY

Another way to use the equity in your home is to sell on the condition you can go on living there, an agreement known as a **sale-leaseback**. You can make your agreement with family members, friends, charities, or commercial investors at whatever price you agree on, often somewhat less than fair market value of your home, for whatever term you like. Often it's 10 to 15 years. However, setting a fair value is important if the buyer is a family

17

Using Your Equity

Your home has financial as well as emotional value.

If you're reluctant to move after you retire, but find that living in your home costs more than you can afford, you can look for ways to use your **equity**, or share of ownership, as a source of cash.

REVERSE MORTGAGES

Reverse mortgages are one way people who own their homes may be able to tap the equity they've built up.

With a reverse mortgage, a bank or other lender sets the amount that you, the homeowner, can borrow. But instead of repaying the lender a fixed amount each month until the loan is paid off and you own the home—as you would with a regular mortgage—just the opposite happens: You borrow against the equity in your home, either on a fixed schedule over a period of years or as often as you need it.

The long-term effect is the reverse of a regular mortgage, too. With a regular mortgage, you build up your equity each time you make a payment. But with a reverse mortgage, your loan balance increases each time you take money.

Because a reverse mortgage is a loan, just the way a regular mortgage is, the lender charges you interest. Sooner or later the lender will want back not only the full amount of the loan, or principal, but also the interest that has built up on the amount you borrowed and any fees that are due.

With a regular mortgage you build up your equity each time you make a payment to the lender.

A bank loans you money to buy a house

Once the mortgage is paid off, you have 100% equity in your house

MORTGAGE TYPES

There are three main types of reverse mortgages: the Home Equity Conversion Mortgage (HECM) insured by the Federal Housing Administration (FHA), the Fannie Mae Home Keeper loan, and the Financial Freedom Cash Account Plan. You can find more details and a list of lenders at www.reversemortgage.com, the website of the National Reverse Mortgage Lenders Association (NRMLA).

THE SCORECARD FOR REVERSE MORTGAGES

PLUSSES	MINUSES
Ready source of cash	Loan must be repaid
No income taxes due on payments because it's a loan, not income	Amount available to borrow may be small
No capital gains tax, though loan amount is based on the current value of your property	Possibility of paying high interest rates, and sometimes high closing costs
No reduction of Social Security payments, since it's a loan, not income	Reduced estate to leave your heirs
Never owe more than value of home at time the loan is due	Could use up loan and still have to move

ARRANGING A DEAL

When you apply for a reverse mortgage, the lender determines how much you can borrow and the interest rate and fees you'll pay. The loan amount is based the value of your house, your equity in it, where you live, the type of loan, and your age. Generally speaking, the older you are, the larger the loan you qualify for.

With a reverse mortgage, your loan increases each time the lender gives you money.

A bank gives you a reverse mortgage based on your equity in the house → **The loan must be repaid when you no longer live in your home**

Since there are only a limited number of lenders, the interest rates and other fees for arranging the loan have tended to be high—something you should watch in negotiating any agreement.

USING THE LOAN

If you arrange a reverse mortgage, you choose the way you want to be able to access the money. These are your choices:

- **Lines of credit, which let you take money from your reverse mortgage account as you need it, usually by writing a check against the available amount**

- **Regular monthly payments, which are the most like a regular mortgage, but in reverse**

- **Lump sum payments, in which you get the total amount of the loan at one time**

- **A combination of monthly income and a line of credit**

A WORD OF CAUTION

Reverse mortgages provide some important consumer protections. For example, the most you can owe when the loan is due is the amount your home is worth. That means if the property loses value between the time you arrange the loan and the date you pay it off, the sale amount will satisfy your obligation to the lender. The same is true if the accumulated interest and fees plus the principal actually equal more than the market value. That's a risk the lender takes.

But there are other risks, which is one of the reasons you're required to talk to a counselor before you can finalize a reverse mortgage. You agree to keep your home in good repair, maintain the insurance, and pay real estate taxes. If you fall behind on these obligations, the lender can require repayment. It is possible that even with the loan you could fall behind and have to sell, leaving yourself with no place to live.

And, if you decide to move after you've agreed to a reverse mortgage, you'll have to repay all the money you received, plus interest, closing costs, and other fees. That could use up most of what you could sell for, making it harder to afford a new place.

LOAN LIMITS

HECM loans, which insure that you'll receive your money if the lender goes out of business and provide inflation protection for your line of credit, have the lowest loan caps. You can borrow more from Fannie Mae and the most with a Financial Freedom Cash Account. But those loans aren't available everywhere.

EQUITY SHARE MORTGAGES

With an equity share reverse mortgage, you can borrow more than you could otherwise and pay a slightly lower interest rate, but you agree to share any increase in your home's value with the lender. The percentage to be shared is set by the terms of the loan.

Making the Move

Some people have their bags all packed, ready to move the day they retire.

Though the statistics show that most people stay put after they retire, you may think of retirement as the time to move to the mountains, the desert, or the beach—or any place away from where you live now. Before you go, you may want to sell your home so you can afford the new life and home you want.

THE COSTS OF SELLING

If you use a real estate agent to sell your house, as most people do, you'll owe a commission, usually 5% to 7% of the sale price. You'll owe your lawyer a fee, too, plus a state transfer tax and your share of the real estate taxes. And you may be responsible for certain closing costs as well, depending on the terms of the sales contract. There's no hard-and-fast rule about who pays for specific expenses like termite inspections or title searches.

There's more flexibility in how much fix-up and repair work you do to make your house attractive to buyers. Some people believe it doesn't pay to put money into the house because the buyers will have their own ideas for improvements. Others argue that buyers respond better to places that look good, and that some new paint and a general fix-up pay for themselves in quicker sales and higher prices.

If there are major problems with the house, though, like a bad roof or an aging furnace, you may have to lower the sales price in negotiating the final contract. You have to gamble on which way you'll come out ahead.

FIGURING CAPITAL GAIN

If you sell your house for more than you paid for it, you may have a **capital gain**. You figure the amount of the gain by subtracting the **cost basis** and the expenses of selling from the price you get. The cost basis is the amount you paid for the house originally, plus what you've invested in improvements. What remains is your gain, also known as your **profit** or your **adjusted sales price**.

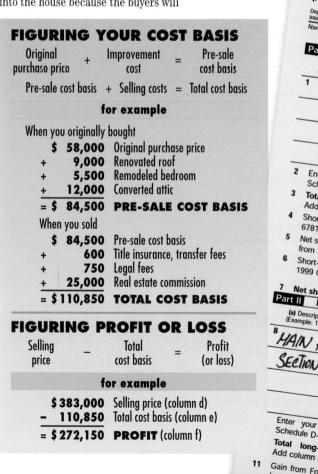

FIGURING YOUR COST BASIS

Original purchase price + Improvement cost = Pre-sale cost basis

Pre-sale cost basis + Selling costs = Total cost basis

for example

When you originally bought

	$ 58,000	Original purchase price
+	9,000	Renovated roof
+	5,500	Remodeled bedroom
+	12,000	Converted attic
=	$ 84,500	**PRE-SALE COST BASIS**

When you sold

	$ 84,500	Pre-sale cost basis
+	600	Title insurance, transfer fees
+	750	Legal fees
+	25,000	Real estate commission
=	$ 110,850	**TOTAL COST BASIS**

FIGURING PROFIT OR LOSS

Selling price − Total cost basis = Profit (or loss)

for example

	$ 383,000	Selling price (column d)
−	110,850	Total cost basis (column e)
=	$ 272,150	**PROFIT** (column f)

SCHEDULE D
(Form 1040)

Department of the Treasury
Internal Revenue Service

Name(s) shown on Form 1040

MARY GAR

Part I Short-Term Capital

(a) Description of property
(Example: 100 sh. XYZ Co.)

1

2 Enter your short-term totals, if
Schedule D-1, line 2 .

3 **Total short-term sales price**
Add column (d) of lines 1 and 2 .

4 Short-term gain from Form 6252 an
6781, and 8824

5 Net short-term gain or (loss) from par
from Schedule(s) K-1

6 Short-term capital loss carryover. En
1999 Capital Loss Carryover Workshe

7 Net short-term capital gain or (loss).

Part II Long-Term Capital Gains a

(a) Description of property
(Example: 100 sh. XYZ Co.)

(b) Date
acquired
(Mo., day, yr.)

8 HAIN HOME   9/1/82

SECTION 121 EXCLUSION

Enter your long-term totals, if any, fr
Schedule D-1, line 9

Total long-term sales price amount
Add column (d) of lines 8 and 9

11 Gain from Form 4797

A TAX BREAK

The IRS offers you a tax break every time you sell your **primary residence**, or a home where you live for at least two of the last five years before you sell. When you sell, the first $250,000 profit is tax free, or the first $500,000 if you're married and filing a joint return. You must wait two years before selling again if you want to enjoy the tax break again.

As an added bonus, you don't even have to report the sale of your primary residence if you satisfy both of the qualifications. However, if you do have a gain and don't meet these qualifications, you should report your gains using Schedule D of IRS Form 1040.

A POTENTIAL PREDICAMENT

If you sold your home before 1997, you had to reinvest the money in a more expensive house within two years to avoid tax on your gain. Many people rolled over real estate profits a few times, continually investing in more expensive property.

If that's your situation, you must decrease the cost basis of the home you are selling by the amount of gain that you deferred on previous sales. If the resulting profit on the current sale is below the tax-

ADVANTAGE: MARRIAGE

You protect twice as much of your profit by selling your home when you can file a joint return, including the year in which your husband or wife dies or in which you get divorced. It probably pays to take such circumstances into account, even if you have other things on your mind. If you've owned your house for several years but have only recently gotten married, you might still investigate your options. There are fewer restrictions on how long you have to be married than on how long you must own your home before selling.

free ceiling, no capital gains tax is due. But if the profit is greater, then the tax is due on the difference. The only good news is that the capital gains tax rate is substantially lower now than it was in the period when you rolled over your gains.

One solution is to leave the home to your heirs, who will inherit it at **a step-up in basis**, which means it would become theirs at its current market price. If they chose to sell promptly, there would be minimal if any gain. On the other hand, capital gains tax rates are significantly less than the estate taxes which might be due if the home increased the value of your estate above the tax-exempt amount.

It pays to get tax and legal advice if you find yourself in this situation.

There's a similar step up with jointly held property. If you sell shortly after your spouse dies, when his or her share has been valued at market rates, you'll have no gain on that part of the property and owe little if any tax. But you may owe capital gains tax on your half.

Capital Gains and Losses

▶ See Instructions for Schedule D (Form 1040).
D-1 for more space to list transactions for lines 1 and 8.

OMB No. 1545-0074

Attachment Sequence No. **12**

Your social security number **123 45 6789**

Losses—Assets Held One Year or Less

Date sold .., day, yr.)	(d) Sales price (see page D-6)	(e) Cost or other basis (see page D-6)	(f) Gain or (loss) Subtract (e) from (d)
2			
3			

gain or (loss) from Forms 4684,

corporations, estates, and trusts | **4**

nt, if any, from line 8 of your | **5**

| **6** (|)

umn (f) of lines 1 through 6 ▶ | **7**

Assets Held More Than One Year

(d) Sales price (see page D-6)	(e) Cost or other basis (see page D-6)	(f) Gain or (loss) Subtract (e) from (d)	(g) 28% rate gain or (loss) (see instr. below) *
383,000 —	110,850 —	272,150 —	
		(250,000) —	

33,000

IF YOU NEED TO REPORT

If your accumulated profit is more than your deduction ($250,000 if filing individually, $500,000 if filing jointly), you'll have to fill out Part II of Schedule D and pay taxes on the difference. You can also find out everything you need to know in IRS Publication 523, "Selling Your Home."

Tax-Deferred Retirement Plans

If you're investing for retirement, consider cultivating a tax-deferred plan.

To help provide the income you'll need later on, you have to invest for retirement while you're working. You can participate in employer sponsored retirement plans, invest in retirement savings plans of your own, or both. What makes these plans different from other types of investing is that your earnings and sometimes your contributions are tax deferred until you withdraw.

GREENBACK QUALIFIED INVESTMENT PLAN

EASY TO PLANT
TAX-RESISTANT

- SOW EARLY AND OFTEN
- CULTIVATE WELL
- GROWTH NOT GUARANTEED

PRIZE-WINNING PLANS

There are many types of employer sponsored plans, and, in general, they work like this: In return for postponing taxes until you start receiving your retirement income, you give up access to the money that's invested.

When employers sponsor retirement plans, they're responsible for making sure their plan meets the legal requirements for the type of plan it is. If you're self-employed, you have the right to set up your own govern-ment approved plan. But you must be sure that the plan follows the rules.

ELIGIBILITY
A plan must offer the same options to everyone who is eligible to participate, and the eligibility rules must be applied consistently.

ANNUAL CONTRIBUTION
There are specific limits on the amount you can contribute each year to employer sponsored, tax-deferred retirement plans.

PAYOUT REGULATIONS
In most cases, you must be 59½ before you start to take income from a retirement plan. In some plans there are limits on the amount you can receive each year. You owe tax on the income at your regular rate.

TYPES OF PLANS

Both employer funded plans and employee contribution plans offer tax-deferred advantages. The major difference from your perspective is the source of the money that's invested—whether your employer puts it in, over and above your salary, or it's taken out of your salary. You may participate in several different plans, either at the same time or at different points in your working life.

Pension plans are funded by your employer, with money that's separate from your salary. Your employer is allowed to deduct the contribution from corporate income tax.

Retirement savings plans are funded with a portion of your earnings. The amount of your contribution is subtracted from the amount reported as income to the IRS, decreasing your current taxes.

Many employers also contribute to your retirement savings plan, often a percentage of your contribution up to a fixed cap.

A Qualified Advantage

When you contribute to a retirement plan, you postpone or defer paying taxes on your contributions and on your investment earnings until you begin to withdraw the money, usually after age 59½. The potentially dramatic difference in growth between a taxable and a tax-deferred investment is illustrated below:

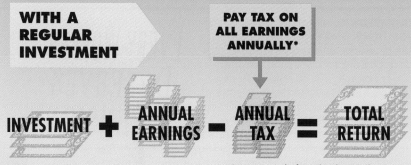

WITH A TAX-DEFERRED PLAN

PAY NO TAX ON CONTRIBUTIONS AND ANNUAL EARNINGS UNTIL YOU WITHDRAW

PAY TAX AS YOU WITHDRAW*

INVESTMENT **+** ANNUAL EARNINGS **=** TOTAL RETURN

* You will owe taxes at your regular rate as you withdraw from your tax-deferred plan.

WITH A REGULAR INVESTMENT

PAY TAX ON ALL EARNINGS ANNUALLY*

INVESTMENT **+** ANNUAL EARNINGS **−** ANNUAL TAX **=** TOTAL RETURN

* Some tax may be figured at the capital gains rate.

OTHER WAYS TO INVEST

A major difference between most employer sponsored plans and other ways to invest for retirement is that your investments in the plan and your earnings are both tax deferred. With the alternatives, such as a nondeductible traditional IRA, a Roth IRA, or a fixed or variable annuity, only the earnings are tax deferred. The one exception is a deductible IRA.

If you're not part of an employer's plan, or you've invested the maximum for the year, one of these after-tax alternatives may be a good choice. But some experts suggest that another way to meet your long-term goals is investing in stocks and other equities in a taxable account. In that case, you'll owe tax on any increases in value and qualifying dividends at the lower capital gains rate.

Pensions

You can collect a pension after you retire—if you work for an employer that provides a pension plan.

Pensions evolved from the belief that employers have an obligation to provide for retired employees who've spent a lifetime working for them. Under traditional pensions, called **defined benefit plans,** employers put money into funds that pay retired workers, and sometimes their survivors, a regular income for the rest of their lives. The amount is usually based on what they were earning and how long they worked.

In recent years, many employers have modified their approach to pension plans. Using **defined contribution plans**, employers put money into pension funds without guaranteeing the retirement benefit employees will receive.

The amount you get from a pension can vary enormously, from a small check at the time you retire to a generous percentage of your final salary every year. The payout depends on the kind and level of plan your employer provides, how well it's managed, and how long you participate.

> **Employer contributions to traditional plans average 10%–12% of your salary. But even the most generous typically put 3%–4% into the increasingly popular 401(k)s.**

WHO'S COVERED... AND WHO'S NOT

Any business that has employees and anyone who is self-employed can set up a pension plan. About 79% of large compa-

nies—with more than 100 employees—and virtually all government agencies provide pension plans for their employees. Only 46% of small companies do, despite the fact that a number of relatively simple plans, including SIMPLEs, are available.

As a result, millions of workers lack the long-term security a retirement plan can provide. Part-time workers are rarely covered by a retirement plan, even when they're long-time employees. The same applies to seasonal workers, and to people who work in low-paying retail and service jobs.

Though there are tax incentives for workers without pension plans to establish individual retirement accounts (IRAs), many don't, either because it doesn't seem important or because they have a hard time putting aside the money they are entitled to invest.

PENSION FINE PRINT

An **integrated plan** is a variation of a pension plan, which can leave you with much less retirement money than you

A HISTORY OF PENSIONS

The first pensions we know about were paid to aged and disabled Roman soldiers when they could no longer fight for the Empire. In the same tradition, military pensions in the U.S. date back to the American Revolution.

By the early 1800s, government workers in several European countries were supported after they retired. The U.S. government introduced pensions in the 1920s to help support retiring civilian employees. Generous pensions, in fact, are a hallmark of public-sector jobs, compensating civil servants for lower salaries than they could earn in the private sector.

The history of most corporate pensions in the U.S. began in the 1930s, and is linked closely to the aftermath of the Depression, the introduction of Social Security, and the influence of labor unions. Where the unions were strong, they fought for employer-funded pensions in contract negotiations. Their successes led to increased benefits for other, non-unionized, workers in those companies.

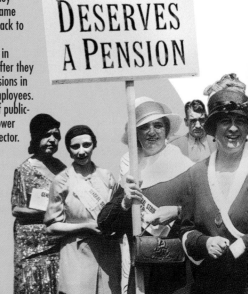

EVERY WORKER DESERVES A PENSION

Two Kinds of Plans

THE COMPANY PUTS MONEY INTO A PENSION FUND IN YOUR NAME

COMPANY A

COMPANY B

DEFINED BENEFIT PLAN

" Company A guarantees you a yearly pension equal to 30% of your salary if you've worked for them for at least 25 years before you retire. "

DEFINED CONTRIBUTION PLAN

" Company B agrees to invest an amount equal to 5% of your salary in your retirement plan each year, and offers you a variety of investment options. "

expected. In an integrated plan, your employer counts a portion of what you get from Social Security as part of your defined benefit—and reduces the amount of your pension accordingly. It's perfectly legal, and it must be explained in the material you're given when you enroll in the retirement plan. But many people miss that detail until it's too late.

PENSIONS AND THE LAW
The federal government does not require companies to provide pension plans, but it does offer an incentive: Companies can deduct the money they pay into a pension fund from their corporate taxes.

At the same time, to help ensure that plans live up to their promises to pay, and to protect tax revenues, the government regulates and monitors them. Unfortunately that oversight has not prevented some plans from failing to live up to their obligations or ensured that all workers who are expecting pensions will receive them. But it has kept the issue in the public eye.

In recent years a number of companies that had traditionally offered plans have

ended them or substituted defined contribution plans.

Some companies have used their pension funds to buy policies with insurers who take over the responsibility of paying retired workers. Others offer bonuses and salary increases instead of retirement account contributions, or give employees a check for the amount accumulated in their pension account.

What these changes mean for the future is that workers will have a much greater long-term responsibility for funding their retirement themselves.

PENSION PLAN LIMITS
The government limits the size of the annual contribution an employer can make to any defined contribution plan to a percentage of your earnings up to an annual cap. Defined benefit plans don't have a contribution limit, but there is a cap on the total amount that an employee can receive from the plan in any single year. It's either 100% of the recipient's average salary or a dollar amount that increases with inflation.

Defined Benefit Plans

Defined benefit pensions are a lot better to look forward to than death and taxes—but they aren't always as certain.

Conventional, employer-funded pension plans, known as **defined benefit plans**, are designed to pay a fixed, pre-established benefit when you retire. If there's a defined benefit plan where you work, you'll probably be included in it if you work full-time. And chances are you won't have many options about how the plan works or how the money is invested. That's the trade-off for the advantages the pension plan provides.

Defined benefit plans generally pay you a regular monthly benefit for your lifetime, sometimes with a final payment to your survivors. In other cases, though, you may be able to choose a lump sum payment when you retire, which you can reinvest. With a generous plan, you might expect an annual income equal to between 30% and 50% of your final salary. But there's no law about how much a pension has to promise to pay, and some workers end up getting very little.

CALCULATING YOUR PENSION

The way your employer figures the amount you get is spelled out in the plan itself. In some plans, for example, there is a standard pension for everyone who meets minimum years-in-service requirements. In others, the annual amount you get reflects what you were earning, with better-paid employees getting higher pensions.

The rules are clear, though, so you can calculate ahead of time what your pension will be. Usually the major factors in determining the amount you'll receive include:

- **Your final salary**
- **The time you've been on the job**
- **Your age**

GETTING ADVICE

Since defined benefit pension plans vary, you need to understand the fine print of any one you're depending on.

Your employer's benefits officer should know the answers to questions like these:

- Is your pension based on your average compensation, your final year's salary, or some other amount?

- Do different length-of-service requirements apply to employees who were hired at different times?

- What's the normal retirement age? What happens to your pension amount if you retire sooner?

- Is there any advantage to working past age 65?

- Is there a COLA?

LONGER IS BETTER

One common formula for finding your pension amount is to multiply the years you've been on the job times a certain percentage, such as 1.5%, and then multiply the result times your final salary.

$$\text{Years on job} \times .015 \ \times \ \text{Final salary} = \text{Pension}$$

for example	
30	Years
x .015	
= .45	
x $ 72,000	Final salary
= $ 32,400	Annual pension

YEARS ON THE JOB

10 YEARS

20 YEARS

30 YEARS

STAYING PUT

Even if you can also count on pensions from a couple of earlier jobs, you may wind up with less retirement income than if you'd been with the same employer for your entire career. That's one reason some workers prefer the more portable defined contribution plans.

EMPLOYER PLANS

BEING VESTED

Being **vested** means you have the right to collect a pension benefit at a specific age, even if you've left the job before then. Without vesting rights, you forfeit any benefit when you leave, and the money becomes part of the general fund.

If you joined a private company plan after 1988, you are vested under one of two minimum schedules. And for contributions in 2002 or later, you are either:

- **100% vested after five years, or**
- **20% vested after three years and fully vested after seven years**

With some employers, you are vested more quickly, and in certain cases you're vested immediately. Some other plans—like a few for government workers

and many teachers—still require you to be on the job for ten years or longer before you're vested.

501 HOURS

If you leave your job before you're vested, you usually lose the credits you've built up toward retirement. But there are ways to keep up your ties and your benefits. One is part-time work. In most cases, working 501 hours a year, the equivalent of 12½ weeks, is enough to keep you on the pension books. However, if you end your career working part-time, your pension will probably be quite small—since your final salary usually determines the amount you get.

You won't lose pension credits, either, if you take up to 501 hours of family leave to care for a new baby or a sick family member.

SALARY	PENSION	
$55,000	**$ 8,250**	
$72,000	**$10,800**	**THE MORE YEARS YOU SPEND ON THE JOB, THE LARGER YOUR PENSION**
$55,000	**$16,500**	
$72,000	**$21,600**	
$55,000	**$24,750**	**TIME ON THE JOB HAS A BIGGER IMPACT THAN FINAL SALARY**
$72,000	**$32,400**	

WHAT'S IN A COLA

Once you retire and your pension is calculated, the amount is usually fixed. Fewer than 10% of private U.S. pensions come with **COLAs, or cost-of-living allowances**, that increase the amount of your pension to keep pace with inflation. Some employers voluntarily increase pensions for retired workers from time to time. Government pensions, on the other hand, are generally adjusted annually to make up for increased living costs.

PENSION

Defined Contribution Plans

The potential risks of defined contribution plans are offset by their potential rewards.

Since the mid-1970s, employers have been increasingly likely to offer **defined contribution pension plans** rather than defined benefit plans. In a defined contribution plan, you, your employer, or both you and your employer contribute to a retirement fund in your name.

There's not a guaranteed pension when you retire. Instead, the amount of retirement income you receive is determined by how much was put into your account, how it was invested, and the return those investments provided. If the economy is healthy and your account does well, you'll be in good shape. But if your account's

performance lags, you could end up with less. There's no way to predict the results until the day you actually retire.

Despite this risk, defined contribution plans do have the potential to provide an even larger retirement income than what you'd get from a defined benefit plan since your income isn't determined by a formula linked to your final salary.

WHO OFFERS THEM?

Some employers offer defined contribution plans, such as profit-sharing, in addition to defined benefit plans. Others have replaced their conventional plans

Types of Defined Contribution Plans

Type	Funding	Contribution
MONEY PURCHASE PLANS	Employer	Employer contributes to plan based on a formula that covers all participating employees
PROFIT-SHARING PLANS	Employer	Employer contributes percentage of profits. Some plans are based on total profits, while others use a sliding scale
THRIFT OR SAVINGS PLANS	Employer and Employee	Employer matches some or all of the amount an employee defers from pretax salary into the plan
401(k) PLANS	Employer and Employee	Employee contributes pretax salary to the plan. Employer may, and often does, contribute an amount based on an announced formula
403(b) PLANS	Employee and sometimes Employer	Employee contributes pretax salary to the plan. Employer may, and often does, contribute an additional amount
SECTION 457 PLANS	Employee	Employee contributes pretax salary to the plan
SIMPLE IRA PLANS	Employer and Employee	Employer must contribute using one of two formulas. Employees may contribute

PACKING YOUR PLAN

Portability is a major attraction of defined contribution plans, along with quicker, or even instant, vesting rights. When you switch jobs, you can often move your accumulated assets to your new employer's plan. That way, you're not starting at pension zero each time you move. If you can't move it, you can often leave your account with your former employer so that it goes on growing until you're ready to retire.

with these more flexible ones. And most employers setting up plans for the first time choose to make a defined contribution rather than provide a defined benefit.

It's easy to see why. Defined contribution plans, though highly regulated, allow employers to shift the burden of making investment decisions and thus the responsibility for determining their own retirement income to their employees. And the plans come in several varieties, giving employers added flexibility in providing benefits.

Some employers offer only one type of defined contribution plan, like a straight profit-sharing plan. These plans are funded by the employer, with the year's contribution tied to how well the company did.

Other employers require employees to contribute a percentage of their pretax income to be included in a retirement plan.

Some of these contribution plans are optional. You get to choose whether or not you want to participate, and how much you want to contribute.

Other employers may also use what's known as **negative enrollment**, though it's not as bad an idea as that term makes it sound. Their employees are automatically signed up to contribute a certain percentage of their salary, commonly 3%, to a retirement plan. They have the choice of staying in or dropping out, and they may change the contribution amount if they wish.

PLAN LOANS

Many defined benefit and defined contribution retirement plans allow participants to borrow against their account balance. Some plans elect not to permit loans even though they could legally do so. But no loans are permitted from IRAs, including accounts you set up for yourself or ones that employers establish, such as SEP-IRAs and SIMPLE-IRAs.

Eligibility	Possible Loan Privileges
All eligible company employees	YES
All eligible company employees	YES
Federal employees and employees of companies offering plans	YES
All employees of businesses and nonprofit employers that sponsor plans	YES
Restricted to employees of nonprofit, tax-exempt employers	YES
Restricted to state and municipal workers	YES
Employees must be allowed to participate if they meet earnings requirements	NO

Salary Reduction Plans

If you want to diversify your retirement fund investments, 401(k)s, 403(b)s, and 457 plans are the right vehicles.

Salary reduction plans are the best-known type of defined contribution plan. And they continue to grow in popularity as more employers offer them and more workers recognize the advantages of making tax-deferred investments when they have the chance.

The 401(k)s, 403(b)s, and 457s—their catchy names are the sections of the tax code that describe them—are also increasingly popular because they are sometimes the only game in town—or at least the only way many employees can participate in a retirement plan.

A Double Plus

The double advantage of tax-deferred plans is saving on your tax bill and investing for retirement

The more money you put in a 401(k) plan...

the lower your taxable salary...

WITH A 401(k) PLAN
you save on taxes while you
invest for retirement

$	75,000	
−	6,000	401(k) investment
= $	69,000	Taxable*

WITHOUT A 401(k) PLAN
you pay more in tax and you
must set aside savings from
after-tax income

$	75,000	
−	0	401(k) investment
= $	75,000	Taxable*

*Before deductions and exemptions

WHAT YOU CAN CONTRIBUTE

The maximum amount you can contribute to a salary reduction plan is set each year by Congress and your employer. The IRS caps the dollar amount, while your employer may impose a restriction based on a percentage of your salary.

For 2004, the government allows you to invest up to $13,000 in a 401(k), 403(b), or 457 plan, and up to $9,000 in a SIMPLE plan. Those caps increase annually to $15,000 for 401(k) and similar plans and to $10,000 for SIMPLEs.

People over 50 can also make annual catch-up contributions designed to boost their account values and provide the potential for greater retirement income.

HOW SALARY REDUCTION WORKS

You invest in a salary reduction plan by having a percentage of your salary deposited in your plan account. The amount you deposit is deferred—it does not count as part of your taxable income for that year.

Employers who offer salary reduction (or salary deferral) plans arrange for you to invest your money in different fixed income, equity, or money market accounts. You choose among the options, and you may pay the costs of investing,

WHEN A 403(b) IS NOT A 403(b)

If you work for a nonprofit organization, you may not recognize the name 403(b), even if you're participating in one. Salary reduction plans are frequently known by other names, including TSAs, tax shelters, and savings plans, especially when they're offered as supplements to defined benefit plans.

such as administrative fees. But you do not have to pay any tax on your contributions to these funds or their earnings until you withdraw from the account.

at the same time. For example, if you're single, make $75,000, and put 8% of your salary in a salary reduction plan, you'll pay $1,350 less in federal income taxes, and you'll have $6,000 growing tax-deferred.

the less tax you pay...

and the greater your earnings potential

$12,000 Taxes on $61,050**

$6,000 earning 8% tax-deferred will grow to $7,560 after 3 years, and $12,960 after 10 years

$13,350 Taxes on $67,050**

**Tax at 2004 rates, single taxpayer, including personal exemption and the standard deduction.

Nothing invested to grow tax deferred and less money to spend

MAXIMUM 401(k), 403(b), AND 457 CONTRIBUTIONS

	People under 50	People over 50
2004	$13,000	$16,000
2005	$14,000	$18,000
2006	$15,000	$20,000

MAXIMUM SIMPLE CONTRIBUTIONS

	People under 50	People over 50
2004	$9,000	$10,500
2005	$10,000	$12,500
2006	$10,000	$12,500

Matching and Switching

Getting the most from your retirement investment requires some fancy footwork.

Many corporate employers who offer salary reduction plans match, or add to, your contribution, up to a limit. A typical formula is to match 50% of what you put in, up to 5% or 6% of your salary. There's also usually a cap on the amount an employer will contribute in each pay period. That means you may end up with more if you spread out your contributions to qualify for matching instead of having your share taken out in larger installments early in the year.

How Matching Funds Work

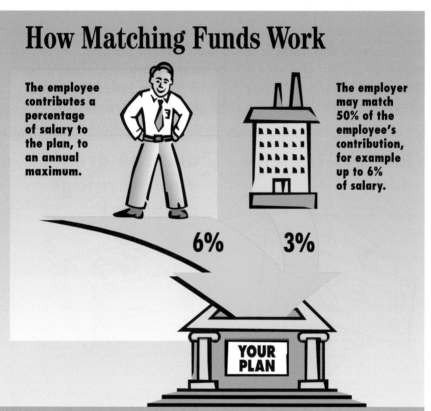

The employee contributes a percentage of salary to the plan, to an annual maximum.

The employer may match 50% of the employee's contribution, for example up to 6% of salary.

6%   3%

YOUR PLAN

The Employee   The Employer

	Contribution	Contribution	
4% of $90,000 salary	**$3,600**	**$1,800**	**50%** of employee contribution
6% of $90,000 salary	**$5,400**	**$2,700**	**50%** of employee contribution
10% of $90,000 salary	**$9,000**	**$2,700**	**50%** of **6%** of employee salary ($5,400)

MOVING THINGS AROUND

Generally, a salary reduction plan lets you put money in as many of the available investment choices as you choose and move your money from one investment to another. Some plans permit only annual transfers, but others allow them quarterly or daily. In some cases, though, there may be surrender fees when you switch between different types of investments.

The reason for using different investment options is to keep your account diversified. Moving assets around works best when you have a strategy for investing your retirement funds, like balancing growth and income. It makes less sense to change investments if you're just trying to guess how the markets will move—called **timing the market**—or you're reacting in panic to a downturn in the stock or bond markets.

THE 403(B) ADVANTAGE

If you work for a college or university, a school system, or other nonprofit group, you may have a choice between a 401(k) or a 403(b), sometimes known as a **tax-deferred annuity (TDA)**. In some cases, the 403(b) option will be the primary retirement plan the employer offers, but in other cases it may be offered as a supplemental salary reduction plan.

While 403(b)s differ in some ways from 401(k)s, you can roll assets from one type into another if you change jobs and your new plan accepts transfers. You can also roll a 403(b) into a 457 plan, or the reverse, under the same circumstances.

You may also have the right to make a tax-free transfer from any investment your 403(b) offers to a mutual fund or annuity of your own choosing as long as you have contributed all the money in the account yourself, and none of it is matching funds from your employer.

The advantage is that you can move money into high-performance, low-fee mutual funds, although making additional investments to the new account may be complicated. And while the transfers may be tax free, they're rarely fee-free.

In addition, some 403(b)s impose steep surrender charges, which can total 7% or more of the assets you're moving, especially on assets in certain fixed-income funds or in fixed or variable annuities.

PASSING THE $90,000 TEST

In addition to the salary limits for figuring contributions, there are rules that govern what percentage of salary employees can contribute to a defined contribution plan like a 401(k). Basically, the rules tie the contributions of employees who make more than $90,000 to the contributions of employees who make less. The rate at which higher-paid employees can contribute is determined by a formula that uses the average percentage contributed by the rest of the employees.

With one formula, if the average contribution for employees earning less than $90,000 is 3% of their salaries, the most anybody earning more can contribute is 5%. In this case, no employee earning more than the $90,000 cut-off could come close to meeting the dollar limit on contributions to salary reduction plans. Someone making $95,000 could contribute $4,750, and someone making $150,000 could contribute $7,500.

IS THE SWITCH WORTH IT?

Switching may be smart, even if you take a big hit on the fees. If the fund or annuity you're moving to has a better track record, or provides greater diversity, than your current provider, the long-term return may be worth the cost of the transfer. But you do have to compare fees carefully, as they can vary significantly.

New participants in 403(b) plans have many more investment choices than were available in the past, so they may be less likely to get caught in the surrender fee crunch than people who began contributing to their plan before 1990, when the IRS issued a ruling making transfers easier.

Paying for the Plans

You should know about the three kinds of fees associated with most 401(k) and other retirement savings plans, since you may be paying some or all of the cost:

- Administrative fees for day-to-day account management

- Investment fees particular to each mutual fund or other investment option that you choose

- Service fees for special features, such as taking out a loan

ADMINISTRATIVE FEES

INVESTMENT FEES

SERVICE FEES

Self-Directed Pension Plans

Contributing to your retirement plan is only the beginning of the story. You're responsible for managing it too.

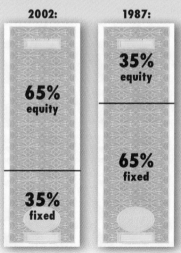

MUTUAL FUND

One major difference between defined benefit and most defined contribution plans is who takes responsibility for making investment decisions. In defined benefit plans, you have no say over where the money goes. But if you contribute to a defined contribution plan, such as a 401(k) or a 403(b), making choices among the investments offered through the plan is entirely your responsibility. The ones you select determine the return that you get. And long term, your choices determine your retirement income.

GROWING CHOICE

Fortunately, you usually have quite a choice. At the minimum you'll be offered three alternatives—such as an equity fund, a fixed-income account, and a money market or other cash equivalent fund. But most plans offer more variety, including mutual funds, annuities, stock purchases, and stable funds. And some plans provide brokerage windows, which allow you to choose among a full range of investments.

401(k) ALLOCATIONS

Between 1987 and 2002, the percentages of 401(k) assets allocated to fixed income and equity were reversed.

2002:

65% equity

35% fixed

1987:

35% equity

65% fixed

Source: Investment Company Institute

FINDING SOLUTIONS

It's smart to make choices for your retirement plan accounts in the context of an overall financial plan. Your investing decisions should take into account your age, other sources of income, and your timeframe for retiring. Here are questions you can ask to help you decide which options you'll choose:

- **What are my investment choices?**
- **What are the objectives of each option, and what are their risks?**
- **How well have the various options been doing over different time periods?**
- **How do the annual expenses compare?**
- **Which choices will help create a balanced and diversified portfolio?**
- **Who pays the investment fees and administrative charges?**

GETTING INVESTMENT ADVICE

Some employers provide very little, if any, investment advice about which options to

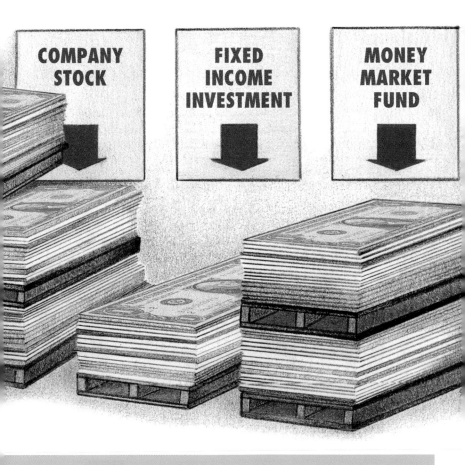

COMPANY STOCK

FIXED INCOME INVESTMENT

MONEY MARKET FUND

SOME DISAPPOINTING RESULTS

Despite the vast sums that employees have contributed to self-directed retirement plans—some current estimates make it close to $2 trillion—financial experts caution that these investments may not produce as much as they should. Three reasons are frequently mentioned:

FEAR OF RISK Employees may not be making the best choices **among the options offered.** They may not realize that in choosing what seems safest, they are limiting their return. That applies, for example, to money invested in fixed income accounts, which are designed to provide guaranteed payments, but have little long-term growth potential.

SHORT-TERM THINKING Investing for retirement requires a long range **view.** Some participants invest as if they need to keep their nest egg available to spend tomorrow. When they do, they often get lower returns and risk losing the fight with inflation. Wise long-term investors, on the other hand, have a better chance of staying ahead of inflation.

NOT ENOUGH DIVERSITY Too many employees put all their eggs in one **basket.** That increases the risk of a major loss if the investment doesn't perform well. By diversifying investments—putting some in stocks, some in bonds, and a little in the shorter-term investments—pension savings have a buffer from periodic ups and downs of any one investment option.

choose or how to allocate your money for the best return. They may fear being held liable if their advice doesn't produce good returns, so they shy away from providing advice at all. In addition, self-directed pension funds may be admin-istered by human resources directors, who are typically not financial managers with expertise in providing investment advice. Whatever the explanation, if you need advice, you may have to get it from other sources.

35

Supplemental Retirement Plans

A company's basic retirement plan may be only the starting point for some employees.

Since the promise of a secure retirement is a way to recruit and keep valuable employees, companies use **SERP**s, or **supplemental executive retirement plans**, to help feather certain nest (egg)s. Despite their potential limitations for both employers and employees, and the fact that contribution limits for qualified plans are going up, these plans continue to be popular.

HOW SERPS WORK

If you're covered by a supplemental plan, it pays to know how they work for you—and sometimes against you. On the plus side, because SERPs are nonqualified plans provided by your employer, there are no limits on the amount that can be contributed. Since you have no access to the money—you can't get it before you leave or retire—you don't owe tax on the contribution until the money is paid out.

THE PROS AND CONS

If your employer offers participation in a SERP rather than a qualified plan, there are some things you should consider. First, you might never collect. Supplemental retirements are paid out of a company's general operating budget, not a special pension fund. Your share is an entry in the company's books, but there's no ownership protection, no insurance, and no government watchdog. So if the company goes bankrupt, or if it's sold, there's no guarantee you'll ever get the money you

Supplementing Your Retirement Plans

WHAT COMPANIES CAN CONTRIBUTE

Supplemental Plans	Standard Plans
The company may provide SERPs, but is most likely to offer them to executives and employees earning high salaries	The company contributes to qualified plans on the same basis for all groups of workers, usually a set percentage of the employee's contributions

SERP

NON-QUALIFIED

QUALIFIED PENSION PLAN

were promised. Some companies, however, buy insurance or set up trusts to protect SERP money.

A second potential problem is how your employer values the growth of your investment. If the money is not actually invested anywhere, it isn't providing a real return. If your employer assumes a fixed income return of around 4%, instead of a well-performing stock fund return, which might be closer to 10%, your account will be worth much less than you might have expected. One solution is for your employer to link the return on your supplemental account to the performance of your 401(k) or some other pension fund.

When you do get the SERP money you were promised, you'll owe tax on the amount. That's because you can't roll the payout over into an IRA or a retirement plan at your new job since SERPs aren't qualified plans.

NEW RULES/NEW WRINKLES

Until recently, SERPs—sometimes referred to as **top hat plans**—were pretty much limited to highly paid executives.

But legislation has limited the top salary on which contributions to qualified pension plans can be figured. As a result, many employers have set up supplemental plans to put more retirement money away for employees who make more than that cap but might not have qualified for special treatment before.

ADDING EXTRA MONEY

Another way to beef up your retirement accounts is to make extra contributions to your 401(k). That means you can contribute the difference between the federal salary reduction limit that's permitted in any one year and your employer's ceiling on contributions, often 15% to 20%.

For example, if your salary is $125,000, a 15% contribution comes to $18,750. So you might add the balance between that amount and the amount of the government's salary reduction cap. Your employer can make additional contributions too.

Like regular 401(k)s, the investment grows tax deferred. But there are some catches:

- Your contribution isn't a salary reduction. You put in money you've already paid tax on

- Your employer's contribution isn't tax-deductible for the firm the way regular retirement contributions are, limiting enthusiasm for matching these funds

- When you begin withdrawals, or if you want to roll over your 401(k) into an IRA, figuring the tax you owe will be more complicated

PLAY CATCH-UP

One of the major changes included in the 2001 tax reform bill is the opportunity for people older than 50 to make catch-up contributions to their salary reduction plans, above the annual limit. The amounts you add as well as any earnings your investment produces are tax deferred. If you can afford to participate, it's probably smart to do it.

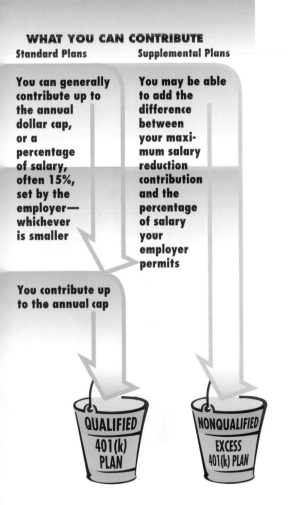

WHAT YOU CAN CONTRIBUTE

Standard Plans

You can generally contribute up to the annual dollar cap, or a percentage of salary, often 15%, set by the employer—whichever is smaller

You contribute up to the annual cap

QUALIFIED 401(k) PLAN

Supplemental Plans

You may be able to add the difference between your maximum salary reduction contribution and the percentage of salary your employer permits

NONQUALIFIED EXCESS 401(k) PLAN

Pension Decisions

When you're mapping out the best route to collecting your pension, there'll be several forks in the road.

Once you've decided to retire, you may have to make a decision about how to collect your pension. The choice is usually between a **lump sum** payment and a lifetime **annuity**, or series of equal or variable payments. The most unnerving element in the process is that once you've committed yourself, you can't change your mind.

If you choose the lump sum, you'll also have to decide what to do with the money. One common option is to put it into an IRA rollover, but you might decide to take a cash payment instead.

THE CRITICAL FACTORS

While you don't have to decide until you're actually ready to stop working, making the best choice is critical. The factors you have to consider are your age and health, what you want to provide for your family, and what other sources of income you'll have. In some cases, too, you have to consider your employer's economic health.

For example, if you're in poor health and concerned about providing for your spouse, a joint and survivor annuity will continue to pay while either of you is alive. On the other hand, if your spouse is seriously ill, you might choose a single life annuity that will provide a larger amount for you each month than a joint annuity would. Usually this requires your spouse's written consent.

HOW TO COLLECT

Individual plans set their own rules for collecting a pension, just as they do for qualifying. You might have to be a certain age, have worked a certain number of years, or a combination of the two.

For example, sometimes you're not eligible to collect a pension until you reach 65, although other plans allow you to begin sooner. The minimum is usually 55—provided you've participated in the plan for at least ten years. If you're younger, you have to wait to collect.

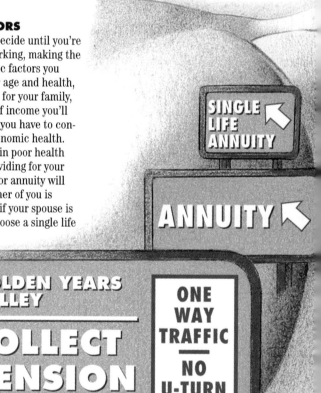

SINGLE LIFE ANNUITY

ANNUITY

GOLDEN YEARS VALLEY

COLLECT PENSION AHEAD

ONE WAY TRAFFIC — NO U-TURN

EMPLOYER PLANS

In most cases, though, your pension is paid when you actually retire. You usually can't postpone the payout, although it may be possible to defer part of it.

DEFINED BENEFIT PENSIONS

Most employers who provide defined benefit pensions provide experts to give you advice on the differences between the payout options. Even though the final decision is yours, the adviser should give you a detailed comparison showing how each option would work and the money you can expect to receive. When you choose, you have to consider not only how much you'll collect, but for how long, and what the tax consequences will be.

A CORPORATE FIRST

Before the 1870s, private companies didn't offer pension plans since most were small family businesses. In 1875, American Express offered the first private pension plan in the U.S. to workers over 60 who had been with the company for 20 years and could no longer work.

While 65 is no longer the hard and fast retirement age it once was, many defined benefit retirement plans are set up as though 65 were still the norm. If you retire earlier, your employer may recalculate the pension you were promised to take into account the added years you'll be collecting instead of working.

If you go on working after 65, federal rules require that your pension keeps on growing until you actually retire and collect on it. That should provide a boost to your income, and perhaps act as an incentive to delay retirement.

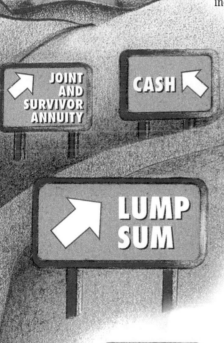

DEFINED CONTRIBUTION PENSIONS

If you have a defined contribution pension plan, you may have similar choices at retirement. You may be able to choose an annuity or periodic payments, or you may prefer a lump sum distribution. Then you are responsible for investing it—perhaps in an IRA—to provide income during your retirement. If you've participated in a stock purchase plan, you can hold onto the shares and continue to collect dividends or sell your shares and reinvest the money. It's wise to consult your professional advisers before you decide.

NO PAYOUT LIMITS

Before 1996, the combined amount you could withdraw from your IRAs and qualified retirement plans each year was $155,000. If you took more, you owed a penalty of up to 15% of the excess.

That limit, however, was eliminated. You can withdraw any amount you wish from your IRAs without penalty. While you'll still owe income tax on your earnings and on any tax-deferred contributions you made to the plans, you won't be penalized for having invested wisely—one of the criticisms that led to the elimination of the penalty. But you may risk running out of money if you take too much during the early years of retirement. If you want more information, get IRS Publication 590 or talk to your tax adviser.

Pension Choices

Understanding the small print helps you balance the pros and cons of payout options.

There's no universal right answer about how to take your pension payout, but when you have to make a decision, it helps to know the advantages—and the disadvantages—of your options.

WHAT THE ISSUES ARE

How comfortable you are with investing money is a major consideration in deciding among the various payout options. If you've been investing successfully for years, the prospect of building your portfolio and your profits with a lump sum pension payout or an IRA rollover can be appealing—and realistic. The challenge, of course, is producing enough income during retirement.

But if you don't want to worry about outliving your assets, you may opt for the relative security of an annuity. Knowing that the same amount is coming in on a regular basis makes budgeting—and occasionally splurging—a lot easier.

Periodic payments offer the same advantages as an annuity—minus the assurance that your income will last your lifetime. But if you feel you'll need the bulk of your pension in the early years of retirement, this could be the wise choice.

You'll also want to weigh the amount you'll owe in income tax. With a lump sum payout, you must pay the total that's due at one time, which can substantially reduce the amount you have left to invest. With the other options, you owe federal income tax at your regular rate as you receive the money.

TAKING YOUR TIME

The good thing about making pension payout choices is that typically you have plenty of time, as retirement doesn't usually take you by surprise. Defined benefit pensions have been in place long enough so that their managers understand the consequences, good and bad, of the various options. Or you can get additional advice from your union representative, tax consultant, or lawyer.

A Close Look At Some

Type		What it is
**ANNUITY**		An annuity is a regular, monthly payment, usually for your lifetime
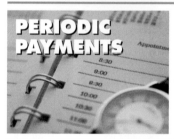**PERIODIC PAYMENTS**		Periodic payments are installment payments of roughly equal amounts paid over a specific period, often 5 to 15 years
**LUMP SUM**		A lump sum is a cash payment of the money in your pension fund
**IRA ROLLOVER**		An IRA rollover is a lump sum payment deposited into an IRA account, which you can either deposit yourself or ask your employer to do directly

PENSION MAXIMIZATION

Pension maximization is salesperson's lingo for a single life annuity repackaged to make it seem more attractive to people trying to get the most out of their pension. With **pension max**, you use part of the higher payment under a single life plan to buy a life insurance policy to cover the needs of the surviving spouse. The consensus is that people are better off in most cases with the choice of a joint and survivor annuity, especially surviving spouses. But some experts believe there may be cases when pension max may make sense. If you're offered this choice, you'll want to weigh the cost of the insurance and the income the survivor will have as you make your decision.

LOCATING THE MISSING

Sometimes pensions get lost in the shuffle—because people forget about them or forget to tell their survivors. Or sometimes a defined benefits plan folds, leaving incomplete records. The Pension Benefit Guaranty Corporation tries to locate the thousands of people each year who are entitled to pensions but aren't collecting. Contact the Pension Benefit Guaranty Corporation at 1200 K Street NW, Washington, DC 20005. The main phone number is 202-326-4000 and the participants number is 800-400-7242. Or you can check the Pension Search listings at their website, www.pbgc.gov.

Important Retirement Choices

Advantages	Drawbacks
● Security of knowing that payments will come in on a regular basis ● Option of spreading the payments out over your spouse's lifetime as well as your own ● Peace of mind in knowing you will have a steady flow of income	● Fixed annuities not indexed for inflation, which means that your fixed annuity will buy less and less as time goes by ● Variable annuities are designed to reflect market performance but produce less predictable returns ● Tax due on the amount you get each year ● You may pay at the highest rate if your pension is generous or you have other sources of income ● Some plans unsafe or underfunded and could fold, leaving you in the lurch
● Assurance of a regular payment at regular intervals ● Relatively large payments because of limited time frame ● Option of rolling some but not all payments into an IRA	● Commitment to payment schedule limits ability to get at lump sum, if needed ● No assurance of lifetime income ● Might leave yourself or spouse without funds after payments end ● Taxes may be due at highest rate ● Inflation can erode purchasing power of payments
● Control over investing and gifting your assets ● Eligible to pay tax on dividends and capital gains at lower long-term gain rate	● Tax due immediately ● Possibility of spending too much too quickly ● Vulnerable to making poor investment decisions ● No assurance of lifetime income—might leave yourself or spouse without funds if assets are exhausted
● Money continues to grow tax-deferred ● Allows you to invest as you want and take money as you need it ● Protection from early withdrawal penalties if you're not yet 59½	● May pay more tax over time than you might have paid on the lump sum ● Withdrawal schedule required after you reach 70½ ● Unless transfer made directly by employer to IRA custodian, 20% of amount is withheld and must be deposited from other sources to avoid being taxed as a withdrawal

Pension Annuities

A pension annuity's distinguishing feature, and its greatest charm, is regularity.

A pension annuity pays you a regular retirement income. It can last your lifetime, or your lifetime plus the life of a survivor. But once you choose, it's set.

GAMBLING ON SURVIVAL

When you choose an annuity, you also have to decide whether you want a **single life** (sometimes called **straight life**) or a **joint and survivor** payout. In a single life annuity, you get a regular payment every month for your lifetime. Basically, the payment is figured by dividing the

amount that has built up in your pension account plus what it is expected to earn over your lifetime by your life expectancy, provided from standard actuarial tables.

If you live longer than statistics predict, you still get your annuity. For example, a woman who retires at 65 can expect to live until she's 85. If she's still collecting her pension when she's 95, the system has worked in her favor. On the other hand, if she dies at 68, the balance in her account reverts—in most cases— to the general pension fund. (There are some exceptions. Certain pension funds make a lump sum payment of the balance of your retirement account to your estate. It's something you should check.)

In a **joint and survivor annuity**, your pension covers your lifetime and the lifetime of your designated survivor—often, but not necessarily, your spouse. The amount of your monthly check is usually less than it would be for a single life annuity. But after one of you dies, the survivor gets a percentage of your pension each month for life. The advantages of the joint and survivor option are clear, especially in cases when your designated survivor is apt to live a long time and doesn't have a separate pension or other income. In fact, the financial benefits that joint and survivor policies provide (for elderly widows in particular) is such a good social policy that the law requires companies to require married employees to choose this option.

THREE KINDS OF ANNUITY PAYOUTS

The chart below compares an example of a single life payout with the amounts you'd get with a 50% joint and survivor annuity and with a 100% annuity. The type of annuity you choose determines the size of your monthly payout. As this example shows, a single life annuity pays the most, but a 100% joint and survivor annuity protects your survivor better.

Type of payout	Retiree's monthly payout UNTIL DEATH	Death of retiree	Spouse's monthly payout STARTING AFTER RETIREE'S DEATH
Single life	$4,167		Nothing
50% joint and survivor	$3,705		$1,853
100% joint and survivor	$3,335		$3,335

The drawbacks of joint and annuity pensions—the smaller payment and the possibility that your survivor might die before you do—are things you have to weigh before choosing this option. But both you and your spouse must agree—in writing—to waive the joint and survivor option if you select a single life annuity or a lump sum payment.

Period certain annuities provide survivor benefits for a set amount of time after the death of the pension holder. Because the payout period is limited—usually to five or ten years—the amount of the basic payment is higher than a joint and survivor annuity. One best reason for making this choice might be to provide short-term support for a younger person, a minor child for example. The limited-term payments can be used to pay college tuition or make the down payment on a house, among other things.

Not all 401(k) and profit-sharing plans offer an annuity option. Instead, they will sometimes make periodic payments, over five, ten, or fifteen years. You can roll over periodic payments into an IRA if they're paid out in fewer than ten years. And you can choose to roll over some of the payments and take the others. That gives you much greater flexibility than you have with defined benefit pensions.

MINIMUM REQUIRED DISTRIBUTIONS

You must begin receiving retirement income from your 401(k) or similar plan by April 1 of the year following the year you turn 70½, unless you're still working.

From 70½ on, you must take at least the **minimum required distribution (MRD)** each year. That amount is calculated by dividing the account balance at the end of your plan's year—usually but not always December 31—by a distribution factor based on your life expectancy.

If your assets remain in the plan, your employer is responsible for making

COMPANY PENSION FUND

COMPANY PENSION FUND

PAY TO THE ORDER OF JOHN J. PENSIONER

THREE THOUSAND TWO HUNDRED

FOR Monthly pension payment No. 00037

The Company

sure that you get at least the minimum amount. The amount is recalculated each year or your employer may use money that has accumulated in your account to buy an annuity contract in your name. Then the insurance company providing the annuity assumes the responsibility for paying you the required minimum each year.

If you prefer, you can roll over the assets in your 401(k) to an IRA. The MRD will still apply once you turn 70½, and you'll be responsible for calculating the amount you must withdraw. One advantage of an IRA is that you can postpone taking income until you do reach 70½. And you can always take more in any one year if you need the money.

Lump Sum Distributions

Sometimes you can take your pension in a lump sum and invest it yourself.

Lump sum suggests the comforting image of a mass of money—a bulwark against financial perils. As you invest it, you hope to shore up the future by beating inflation, which causes fixed income to lose its value. What's more, you don't have to worry about the pension plan going bust or your former employer changing pension policy. But you do need to be concerned about decreasing assets.

HOW LUMP SUM PAYMENTS WORK

When you take a lump sum distribution from a defined benefit plan, your employer figures out how much you would get if the plan paid you an annuity over your projected lifespan, and then calculates how much the pension fund could have earned in interest on that amount during the years of your payout. Your lump sum share is what you would have been entitled to, reduced by a factor of the projected interest earnings known as the **discount rate**.

If interest rates are high, your lump sum will be less than in a period of low interest. That's because the pension fund hates to give up any money-producing investment—in this case your share of the plan assets. Once you have the lump sum, the responsibility for investing it to make it last through your retirement is yours.

MAKING IT LAST

In contrast, if you take a lump sum payout from your defined contribution plan, the assets in the plan are sold and the cash, minus transaction costs, is yours. The amount that has been invested and the return those investments have provided determine the value of your account.

The current state of the investment markets matters here as well. In a flat or falling market, your payout will be less than in a growth phase. The one advantage of a smaller account value is a smaller tax bill.

IT'S YOURS—NOW

You can take a lump sum distribution in cash—or perhaps more precisely by check or direct deposit. Or you can roll over the money into an **individual retirement account (IRA)**. With a rollover, you preserve the tax-deferred status of your account. But if you take the cash, tax on the entire amount will be due in the year you receive the money.

CASH DISTRIBUTION

ADVANTAGES	DRAWBACKS
● Can use money immediately	● Easy to spend too fast
● Can invest to take advantage of lower long-term capital gains rate	● Taxes due immediately
	● Must make initial investment decisions quickly
	● Earnings on assets no longer tax deferred

COMPARING EARNINGS

Unless you plan to spend the bulk of your pension payout right away—a decision you'll want to weigh carefully unless you have other sources of retirement income—you have the opportunity to roll over the account value into either a traditional or Roth IRA. If you choose the traditional account, no tax is due on the amount you move. You can either make the transfer into an existing IRA or open one or more new ones, either to make different types of investments or to name different beneficiaries for each account.

Or, if you prefer, you can pay the income tax that's due, just as you would if you were taking the cash, and roll the balance into a Roth IRA. There is an income limit on eligibility: Your adjusted gross income can't be more than $100,000, not including the amount you're moving, whether you file your tax return as a single or jointly.

The advantage of the Roth IRA is that withdrawals are tax free if you're older than 59½ and your account has been open five years or longer. So it may turn out you pay less tax overall. What's more, withdrawals aren't required, so you have more flexibility in deciding when to use these assets.

LUMP SUM

IRA ROLLOVER

MOVING TO AN IRA ROLLOVER

You can move the money from your retirement account to an IRA in two ways:

- **You can get a check for the money, just as you would if you were taking a lump sum payout and deposit the full amount in the IRA within 60 days**

- **You can have the money transferred directly to the trustee or custodian of your new IRA**

The advantage of taking the cash is that you can use the money for 60 days before the deposit deadline. That flexibility can be outweighed by the fact that your employer must withhold 20% of the amount before writing you a check. You get the 20% back when you file your income tax return for the year, but not quickly enough to meet the deadline. That means you have to come up with money from other sources so you can put the full amount in your IRA. Any amounts you don't deposit within the time limit are considered withdrawals and taxed at your regular rate. If you're younger than 59½, you may also owe a 10% penalty in addition to the taxes. The exception is if you're over 55 and stop working. Then the penalty is waived.

When the money is transferred directly, nothing is withheld, and you don't have to worry about missing the 60-day deadline. That makes it the method of choice for many people. It can also reduce any temptation to spend the money.

You can withdraw from your IRA without penalty once you reach 59½, and at 70½ you'll have to begin taking minimum required distributions (MRD). Or, if you take another job you many be able to move the assets in the IRA into your new employer's retirement plan.

ADVANTAGES	DRAWBACKS
● Defer taxes until you withdraw funds	● May pay more taxes in the long run
● Make investment decisions at your own pace	● Responsible for your investment decisions
● Eligible for tax-deferred growth	● Must begin withdrawals by 70½

INVESTING A LUMP SUM

One challenge in investing a lump sum payment is how to put your assets to work without feeling that you're rushing or making snap decisions. It is true that the sooner you invest, the more potential your principal has to grow. But that advantage can disappear if you haven't developed a strategy for building a diversified portfolio and selecting appropriate investments.

One approach, if you aren't planning to begin taking income from the investment in the next few years, is to buy stocks and bonds, either directly or through exchange traded funds (ETFs), mutual funds, or managed accounts, for a combination of income and long-term growth. If those investments perform as you expect, you can sell them at a profit at some point in the future. Then you'll owe tax at the lower long-term capital gains rate rather than at your regular income tax rate.

On the other hand, if you want to invest to produce current income, you might consider putting some of the payout into municipal bonds. Though the interest rate these bonds pay is typically lower than what you could earn on similarly rated corporate bonds, the income is free of federal tax and, in some cases, of state and local tax as well.

STOCK DISTRIBUTIONS

If your qualified plan includes stock your employer contributed, consider taking the stock as a lump sum distribution instead of rolling it into an IRA. You'll pay income tax on your **basis**, or the stock's value when it was added to the account, and capital gains tax if you sell. But that could cost you less than paying income tax at your regular rate on the stock's increased value as you withdraw from your IRA.

Changing Jobs, Changing Pensions

Retirement savings are portable…if you know what you have to move and where to store it

If you change jobs—many people do every three to four years—protecting your retirement pension and investments may require some tough choices. Of course, what you can do depends on the type of plan, or plans, you've participated in. Sometimes your employers make all the decisions. But in many cases you'll be responsible for choosing a new home for the money. Even if you're short of cash, the biggest mistake you can make is spending it. You'll need it more after you retire.

CHOOSING WISELY

As a rule, if you're part of a 401(k), a profit-sharing plan, or a money purchase plan, you can get a lump sum distribution of the money that's been invested in your name, plus whatever the investment has earned. Then you'll have to decide what to do with the money, before taxes gobble up a big share of it. The chart below summarizes the details of the most frequent options.

Your options and their consequences

OPTION	TAX CONSEQUENCES	PLUSES AND MINUSES
Transfer money directly to IRA	None	Rollover assets eligible to roll into future employer's plan if new plan accepts rollovers
Roll distribution into IRA yourself	20% withheld. Total amount must be deposited within 60 days, including the 20%, or subject to tax and 10% penalty if younger than 59½	Gives you short-term access to money, with potential penalties
Begin periodic withdrawals	Tax on distributions, but no early withdrawal penalty	Distributions must continue for five years or until 59½, whichever is longer Depletes money earmarked for retirement
Leave money in former employer's plan (not always an option)	None	Investment continues to grow undisturbed and can be later rolled into an IRA or moved to new employer's plan
Take cash as lump sum	Taxed as current income, plus 10% penalty if younger than 59½	Flexibility to use some cash and roll rest into an IRA Lose ability to roll money into new employer's plan Risk depleting retirement savings

AVOIDING THE HASSLE

Some retirement plans, aren't tied to a particular employer. If you move from one institution to another, your pension goes with you. And if you're vested, but change careers, the amount in your plan continues to grow tax-deferred.

Some civil service pensions offer reciprocity: Pension contributions you make as a state employee and time spent on the job count if you move to a federal job, or vice versa. A state police officer, for example, who joins the Secret Service, begins the new job with a pension credit already on the books.

RESTRICTED RIGHTS

If you're part of a defined benefits plan, your employer usually won't offer a lump sum when you leave, and won't start paying you a pension until you reach the minimum age for early retirement—sometimes 55, but often older. Then you're eligible for what accumulated up to the time you left, either in a lump sum or as an annuity.

Thanks to changes in vesting rules, you probably will be entitled to the money your employer has contributed to the plan. But if you change jobs at 40, and can't collect for 15 or 20 years, don't expect the pension to pay a lot. In some cases, your account will have been frozen, so no investment earnings will be credited to your account after you left the job. And inflation will eat away the value of the money you do eventually receive.

HANDLING THE DETAILS

If your pension has included a stock purchase plan, or if your employer has contributed stock to a profit-sharing plan, you can hold onto it since it's in your name, or sell if the price is right. If you hold onto the stock, you can continue to use your former employer as your agent, or take the stock as a lump sum distribution and hold it in a brokerage account. The advantage of a broker can be easier access, and possibly smaller commissions when you do decide to sell.

If you're leaving a 401(k), you may have to turn your other investments into cash before you can move them.

EARLY RETIREMENT PACKAGES

Sometimes employers offer incentives for retiring early, like adding three to five years to the years you've actually worked, or increasing the percentage of salary your pension will replace. Together, the incentives could mean a significantly bigger retirement income.

Or your employer may offer you a lump sum payment on top of the pension you would receive if you retire early—like a week's pay for each year you've been on the job.

If you have a choice between a bigger pension or **severance**, a bonus for leaving, multiply the increase in monthly pension you've been offered times your life expectancy, and compare that figure to the amount of the severance offer.

For example, if at age 55 you're offered a $75,000 severance or $500 a month added to your pension, you'd probably make out better with the pension:

Added pension	x	Life expectancy	=	Value of pension
for example				
$ 500		Added per month		
x 12		Months		
= $ 6,000		Added per year		
x 30		Years		
= $ 180,000		Value of increased pension		
− 75,000		Severance offered		
= $ 105,000		Additional retirement income		

Pensions: Money Problems

Whether a pension fund is underfunded or overfunded, the result may be severely reduced pensions.

When pensions work the way they're supposed to, they help insure the financial security of millions of retired workers. But there can be major headaches for people who are counting on that income if a pension doesn't deliver what it promises.

That can happen if a pension is **underfunded**. Underfunding means that there's not enough money in a pension account to pay retiring employees.

There can also be problems if the pension fund is **overfunded**. While on the surface it seems as if having more money than you need should be a positive rather than a negative sign, overfunding has problems of its own.

For example, employers with overfunded plans may reduce their estimates of what they'll owe or increase their projections of what they'll earn. In an economic downturn, they can suddenly turn out to be short on the cash they need.

Underfunded means that a pension is short on the money it needs to meet its projected expenses

BOTH PUBLIC AND PRIVATE PENSION FUNDS CAN BE UNDERFUNDED

Overfunded means that a pension has more funding than it needs to meet projected expenses

OVERFUNDING LIMITS A COMPANY'S ABILITY TO ADD TO ITS PENSION FUND

SHORT ON MONEY

Private plans may come up short if:

- **The plan's investments don't do as well as expected**
- **The employer simply doesn't contribute enough**
- **The employer borrows the money to expand or bail out a faltering business and doesn't—or can't—replace it**

Public pension funds can be underfunded because state and local governments are reluctant, in the face of increasing opposition, to raise taxes enough to meet their projected obligations. Some states have also tried to use the contributions they should be making to the pension fund to meet short-term obligations.

LOOKING FOR A WAY OUT

As more and more people reach retirement age, many private employers have cut back on pension promises to newer employees, renegotiated existing obligations, increased the use of defined contribution plans (which can't be underfunded), and ended their defined benefit plans altogether. Health insurance coverage has also been radically reduced or eliminated, even for former employees who have already retired.

ERISA, the Employee Retirement Income Security Act, does protect employees to some extent. If the plan where you work is ended, your employer must provide the money you're entitled to at that point, by buying you an annuity or

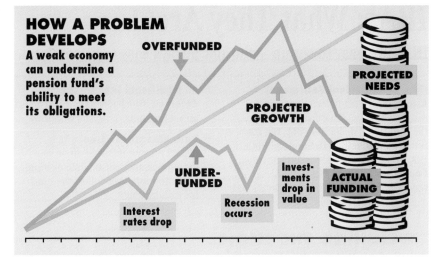

HOW A PROBLEM DEVELOPS
A weak economy can undermine a pension fund's ability to meet its obligations.

OVERFUNDED

PROJECTED GROWTH

PROJECTED NEEDS

UNDER-FUNDED

Invest-ments drop in value

ACTUAL FUNDING

Recession occurs

Interest rates drop

---

making a lump sum payment. But neither of those is likely to provide the same level of long-term income a pension would provide.

SWITCHING PLANS
In recent years, some employers have converted their traditional pension plans to cash balance plans. Though legally a defined benefit pension, **cash balance plans** share some characteristics with defined contribution plans. When you leave a job or retire, you may move or withdraw the balance that has accumulated in your name or choose a lifetime annuity. The annuity payment is based on what has accumulated in your account, not on a formula based on what you've earned or how long you've worked.

The controversy associated with switching from traditional to cash balance fund is that long-time workers often get a smaller pension than they would have qualified for had the traditional plan continued.

CHECKING UP
Contact the Pension Rights Center at www.pensionrights.org, or at the address above for answers to some of your pension questions. For information closer to home, you can ask your employer for a copy of Form 5500, which has to be filed every year with the government, reporting on the plan's investments and its financial health.

MAKING NOBODY HAPPY
State and local governments, which have depended on the promise of generous pensions instead of high salaries to make themselves competitive with the private sector in attracting qualified workers, are also looking for ways to reduce their pension obligations.

One solution has been to make the biggest cuts in benefits to people working fewer than ten years, or to require them to work more years to qualify. Other approaches have been to increase the amount workers must contribute themselves to pension plans, to limit cost-of-living increases, and to reduce the use of overtime to boost final-year salaries that are the basis for pension payouts. Elected officials, though, must weigh the political cost of public employee anger against the consequences of imposing higher taxes.

Public pension plans are not covered by ERISA, so they can make more radical changes than private plans can, including cutting or delaying benefits.

PENSION GUARANTEES
The Pension Benefit Guaranty Corporation, established in 1974, guarantees pension payments to approximately 40 million workers who are covered by 85,000 defined benefit plans. The PBGC doesn't promise you'll get the full amount you planned on, but it does guarantee that you will get something.

Pension Rights Center
1350 Connecticut Ave. NW
Washington D.C. 20036

IRAs: What They Are

IRAs are easy to set up—but not always easy to understand.

IRAs, or Individual Retirement Accounts, are tax-deferred, personal retirement plans. There are three types: the traditional deductible IRA, the traditional nondeductible IRA and the Roth IRA. (Education IRAs, recently renamed **Education Savings Plans (ESA)**, are a way to accumulate money for educational expenses, not retirement plans.)

- All **traditional IRAs** are **tax deferred**, which means you owe no tax on your earnings until you withdraw
- **Roth IRAs** are **tax free**, which means you owe no tax at all on your earnings as they accumulate or when you withdraw, if you follow the rules for withdrawing

WEIGHING THE CHOICE

If you have a choice of which IRA to open, you'll want to weigh the pros and cons:

	ROTH	TRADITIONAL IRA	
		Nondeductible	**Deductible**
PROS	• Tax-free income • No required withdrawals	• Tax-deferred earnings	• Immediate tax savings on tax-deferred investment • Tax-deferred earnings
CONS	• Not deductible • Account must be open five years to qualify for tax-free provision	• Not deductible • Tax due at regular rates at withdrawal • Required withdrawals beginning at 70½	• Tax due at regular rates at withdrawal • Required withdrawals beginning at 70½

DO YOU QUALIFY FOR A ROTH IRA?

Single

You don't qualify for a Roth

$110,000 _____

Partial Roth

$95,000 _____

You qualify for a Roth

Adjusted Gross Income

Married

You don't qualify for a Roth

$160,000 _____

Partial Roth

$150,000 _____

You qualify for a Roth

Adjusted Gross Income

A SWEET DEAL

The only requirement for opening an IRA is having earned income—money you get for work you do. Your total annual contribution is limited to $3,000, increasing to $4,000 for 2005, whether you put it all in one account or divide it between a traditional IRA and a Roth. If you're over 50, you can also make annual catch-up contributions of $500.

Any amount you earn qualifies, and you can contribute as much as you want, up to the cap. But you can't contribute more than you earn. For example, if you earn $1,800, that's how much you can put in.

SPOUSAL ACCOUNTS

If your husband or wife doesn't work, but you do, you can put up to the annual limit into a separate spousal account. The advantage for the nonworking partner is being able to build an individual retirement fund.

WHICH IRA FOR YOU?

If you qualify for all three types of IRAs, based on your **adjusted gross income** (AGI), you'll have to choose among a traditional deductible IRA, a traditional nondeductible IRA or a Roth IRA.

The traditional deductible IRA has the strictest limits, and the traditional nondeductible has none at all. The Roth, which many experts describe as the best deal for most people, is in between.

In 2004, for example, you can deduct all of your IRA contribution if you're single and your AGI is less than $45,000, a gradually

decreasing portion as your income gets closer to $55,000 and nothing if it's above $55,000. You can always deduct the full amount of your contribution if you're not covered by a retirement plan at your job.

You're eligible for a full Roth if you're single and your AGI is less than $95,000. With an AGI between that amount and $110,000, you can put a portion of your contribution into a Roth.

For a married couple, the limits for a deductible IRA are $65,000, phased out at $75,000. Either of you can deduct if you have no retirement plan of your own at work. But if your spouse has a plan,

your right to a deduction is reduced gradually if your joint income is over $150,000 and eliminated if it's over $160,000. The Roth limits are $150,000, phased out at $160,000 for couples filing a joint return. If you file separate returns, you can't contribute to a Roth.

IT'S YOUR ACCOUNT

It's easy to open an IRA. All you do is fill out a relatively simple application provided by the bank, mutual fund company, brokerage firm or other financial institution you choose to be **custodian** of your account.

Because IRAs are self-directed, meaning that you decide how to invest the money, you're responsible for following the rules that govern the accounts. Basically, that means putting in only the amount you're entitled to each year and making approved investments. You must also report your contribution to the IRS, on your basic return if it's deductible and on Form 8606 if it's not.

You can invest your IRA money almost any way you like, from putting it in sedate savings accounts to buying volatile options on futures. The only things you can't buy are fine art, gems, non-U.S. coins and collectibles. And you can buy and sell investments in your IRA account whenever you please without worrying about paying tax on your gains until you withdraw from your account.

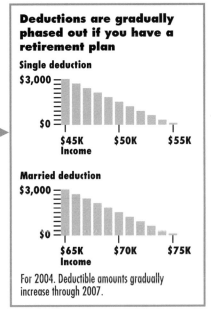

Deductions are gradually phased out if you have a retirement plan

Single deduction

$3,000 — ... — $0

$45K $50K $55K
Income

Married deduction

$3,000 — ... — $0

$65K $70K $75K
Income

For 2004. Deductible amounts gradually increase through 2007.

You have until April 15—the day taxes are due—to open an IRA account and make the deposit for the previous tax year.

You can contribute to your IRA in a lump sum or spread the deposit out over the 15 months. You get the best return on your investment if you put in the whole amount the first day you can, January 2 of the tax year you're making the contribution for. If you're like most people, you're more apt to make the deposit the last possible day. The most practical solution may be weekly or monthly contributions.

WHEN TO CONTRIBUTE

January 2
Best day to deposit lump sum

April 15
Last day to deposit lump sum

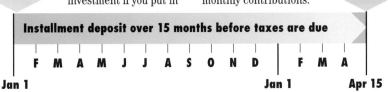

Installment deposit over 15 months before taxes are due

F M A M J J A S O N D | F M A

Jan 1   Jan 1   Apr 15

IRAs: Your Show

You call the shots on your IRA, so it helps if your goals are clearly in focus.

Since IRAs are designed to be long-term investments, and can play an important part in insuring a secure retirement, you'll want to have a plan for building your account. The first rule is to **diversify**, which means spreading your money among several different types of investments. That way

you reap the returns on investments that are performing well and protect yourself against the risk of depending on just one investment category.

One strategy is to use some of your IRA to buy investments that return the highest income. Since it's a tax-deferred account, you don't have to worry about increasing your tax bill. And you can use the income to make additional investments.

Another approach is to buy riskier investments, like small-company stocks or aggressive mutual funds, early in your career and gradually shift them to income producing investments as you get closer to retirement. If they have a long time to grow, they may increase the value of your account more rapidly than more conservative investments.

QUESTIONABLE CHOICES

Are there any investments to avoid in your IRA? Experts have different points of view on the subject, but many agree that there are good arguments against:

- Low-paying savings and other cash accounts because they're unlikely to provide enough return for long-term growth
- Municipal bonds because they lose their tax-free advantage in a traditional IRA since all withdrawals are taxed at your current tax rate

Opinion is mixed on putting IRA money into variable annuities. The ayes stress that annuities have real earnings potential. The nays argue that since annuities are already tax deferred, you may end up paying extra fees for no added benefit.

SAVING ON FEES

Consolidating your IRA accounts with a single custodian can save you money, because you generally pay an account fee of between $10 and $50 to maintain each IRA. The fee's the same whether you have $2,000 or $20,000 in the account. But some custodians waive the fee entirely if your combined account with them is large enough, usually over $10,000.

You can let the bank or mutual fund deduct the fee from your account, or you can write a separate, tax-deductible check to cover it. That way, your entire investment can go on growing.

KEEPING TRACK OF YOUR IRAS

While you can set up a different IRA every year, keeping track of your accounts can be a nightmare long before you begin figuring your withdrawals. That's another argument for using one broker, bank or mutual fund as the custodian. You can have several different types of investments, but your records will be on one statement that provides all the information you need.

Since you might have several different types of IRAs in your lifetime—deductible, nondeductible and Roth—it's especially important to keep good records. For example, you don't want to end up paying taxes twice on nondeductible contributions you've made, as you might if you didn't have records to show their status. The catch is that you probably need to hold onto the paperwork for as long as you have your IRAs.

A RECIPE FOR TROUBLE

As important as it is to keep your records straight, consolidating your accounts isn't always the solution. Your Roth IRAs must be held separately from your traditional ones, and your deductible and nondeductible accounts should be separate as well. That's because when it's time to withdraw, figuring the tax you owe can be a problem.

For example, if, by the time you retire, you have put $40,000 in IRAs—$16,000 in deductible contributions and $24,000 in nondeductible—and they've produced $56,000 in earnings, how do you figure the tax that's due?

TAXES ON LUMP SUM WITHDRAWAL

	$ 96,000	Total value of IRA
−	24,000	Nondeductible contributions
=	$ 72,000	Taxable part of lump sum

THERE'S A HITCH—OR TWO

Chances are you aren't going to withdraw your IRA money in a lump sum. That means you have to figure out what percentage of the money that has already been taxed is included in each withdrawal, and compute the tax you owe on the balance. Using the same example, you can figure out the taxable part of a $3,000 withdrawal in two steps, finding the taxable percentage and the taxable amount. It won't work to say you're using up the nondeductible portion of your savings first. The IRS says you must treat withdrawals as if they came from all your IRAs proportionally, even if you have always kept the accounts separate and actually withdraw from just one.

TAXES ON A $3,000 ANNUAL WITHDRAWAL

Step one:

	$ 24,000	Nondeductible contributions
÷	96,000	Total value of IRA
=	25%	Nontaxable percentage

Step two:

	$ 3,000	Total value of withdrawal
x	.25	Nondeductible percentage
= $	750	Is nontaxable, so you owe tax on $2,250

INVENTING IRAS

IRAs were created on Labor Day 1974 when President Ford signed the Employee Retirement Income Security Act (ERISA). The story has it that the committee designing the plan to encourage personal savings struggled to find a name with a pronounceable acronym—and borrowed their solution from Ira Cohen, the IRS actuary who was working with them.

IRAs: Weighing the Merits

It's hard not to love your IRA, and it's smart to understand it.

The tax-deferred advantage of an IRA is that your investment can compound much faster than it would in a taxable account, as this hypothetical example shows.

$46,000

START CONTRIBUTING AT AGE 18

If you contributed $3,000 a year for ten years as soon as you started earning, and then stopped contributing, your $30,000 investment would go on growing until you were ready to withdraw. Even then anything left in the account would continue to grow tax deferred.

STOP CONTRIBUTING AT AGE 28

If you earned 8% a year on the investment, you would have $46,936 in the account when you stopped putting money in at the end of ten years.

TAXING ISSUES

Traditional IRAs and the newer **Roth IRAs** both give you the advantage of **tax-deferred** growth. What's different is what happens when you take money out of your account after you reach age 59½.

With a traditional account, what you withdraw is considered regular income, and you owe income tax on the earnings at your current rate. If you've deducted your contributions, you owe tax on that part of your withdrawal as well. As a result, the amount you have available to spend is reduced by whatever you owe in tax.

Withdrawals from a Roth account are completely **tax free** if your account has been open at least five years. That's a big difference that gets bigger as your tax rate goes higher. For example, if you were single and withdrew $40,000 in one year, you would have about $6,700 more in your pocket (at 2004 rates) if the money came out of a Roth account.

ADDED APPEAL

Roth IRAs offer other advantages, too, if you're eligible to open one, based on your income. Unlike a traditional IRA, you can continue to contribute for as long as you have earned income—even if you're 90.

Perhaps more important, you're not required to begin withdrawals at age 70½ as you are with a traditional IRA. That means you can manage your finances to suit yourself, or use your account to build the estate you'll leave your heirs. There

may be tax consequences with that approach, though, so you should discuss your plans with your tax or legal adviser.

If there's a drawback to Roth IRAs, it's that the contribution is never deductible. But experts agree that for most people long-term tax-free income will have more advantages than a deduction now.

Another alternative is to put growth investments in a regular, taxable account. The capital gains tax rate when you sell them is only 15%—or 5% if your regular rate is 10% or 15%.

THE PENALTY QUESTION

To get the tax breaks that come with an IRA, you're accepting the condition that you won't have access to the money until you reach age 59½. It's the government's way of encouraging you to save for retirement. In fact, sometimes you have to pay a 10% withdrawal penalty on top of the tax due when you take money out ahead of schedule.

But the law is also flexible. If you need money you've put into an IRA to pay certain medical expenses, buy your first home or pay your children's college tuition, you can withdraw from your account without owing the 10% penalty that usually applies to early withdrawals.

TIME TO START AGAIN
If you stopped contributing to your IRA when the deductibility rules changed in 1986, should you reconsider? Many financial advisers think so, especially if you qualify for a Roth.

A $30,000 investment can provide a $1.28 million resource

WAIT UNTIL AGE 70½

When you reached 70½, your account would be worth $1,285,000. That's enough to pay you roughly $85,000 a year for 15 years, or just over $50,000 a year for 25 years.*

*This result is not based on the performance of any specific investment.

If the money is coming out of a traditional IRA, you'll owe whatever tax is due, just as you would if you withdrew after age 59½. But you'll have the rest to spend on those important expenses. With a Roth, you'll owe tax at your regular rates for earnings you withdraw to pay college expenses. But you can take up to $10,000 tax free if you're buying a first home for yourself, your child or your grandchild.

There's general agreement that flexibility is good. But is withdrawing early a smart move? Those who say it's not point out that you run the risk of not having enough to live comfortably in retirement—at a time when it's often harder to borrow or to work extra hours for added income. In addition, since **compounding** is the key to maximum growth, you won't be able to accumulate as much if you start rebuilding an account at age 40 or 50 as you would if your money grew uninterrupted.

IRA FEES

IRAs cost little or nothing to set up and aren't expensive to maintain. Banks rarely charge fees at all. Mutual funds and brokerage firms may charge between $5 and $50 to open your account and often a similar annual fee, although sometimes they'll waive the charges to attract or keep your business, especially if you have a sizeable sum.

Since some of the fees are fixed, and not based on the size of your IRA, they have a much smaller impact than the fees

often imposed on other retirement savings plans. And you can subtract the annual fee as a miscellaneous deduction on your income tax return if you pay the fees by check rather than having them deducted from your account.

But the annual fees don't cover sales charges or commissions on the buying and selling you do within your IRA. Those costs can't be paid separately. They are based on the size of each transaction, and are not tax deductible.

NO LONGER AN IRA?

Education IRAs once shared a name with traditional and Roth IRAs. They also share the benefit of tax-deferred growth. And, with a Roth, they share the opportunity for tax-free withdrawals. But they're not really IRAs in the customary sense, since they're designed to help pay educational expenses. So they've been renamed Coverdell education savings accounts (ESAs).

While the tax advantages are a plus, there are some limitations with ESAs, including:

- Each ESA must be set up for a specific beneficiary (though the money can be used for another member of the family under certain conditions)
- Annual contributions are limited to $2,000 per beneficiary a year
- There's an adjusted gross income cap limiting who can make contributions

IRA Rollovers

Rollovers are a hop, skip, and a jump from conventional IRAs.

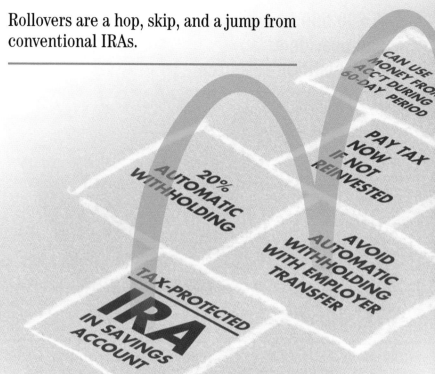

CAN USE MONEY FROM ACC'T DURING 60-DAY PERIOD

PAY TAX NOW IF NOT REINVESTED

20% AUTOMATIC WITHHOLDING

AVOID AUTOMATIC WITHHOLDING WITH EMPLOYER TRANSFER

TAX-PROTECTED IRA IN SAVINGS ACCOUNT

You can move money in one traditional IRA to another traditional IRA without penalty, and without owing any tax on the earnings that have accumulated. You can move the money yourself, by getting a check for the amount in the IRA you're closing and depositing that check with the custodian of your new IRA. What you're doing is called rolling over your IRA. Or you can have the custodian of the existing IRA send the money directly to the custodian of the new IRA.

If you roll over one traditional IRA to another traditional IRA or one Roth to another Roth, you have 60 days from the time you take the money out of the existing account to deposit it in the new account. If you miss the deadline or deposit only a portion of what you withdrew, you owe income tax on the amount you don't deposit and potentially a 10% early withdrawal penalty if you're younger than 59½.

ROLLOVER IRAs

You may also move assets in a employer sponsored retirement plan, such as a 401(k), Keogh, or pension, into an IRA if you retire, change jobs, or the plan ends. Moving the money to an IRA means that your retirement savings can continue to accumulate tax deferred until you are

ready to begin withdrawals. The IRA you open in this situation is called a rollover IRA.

As always, there are rules

Like IRAs you roll over from one account to another, rollover IRAs funded with retirement plan money are subject to some specific regulations. Following the rules postpones taxes and protects you from fees and penalties.

1 DEPOSIT WITHIN 60 DAYS

First and foremost, the 60-day rule applies. If you put your retirement plan payout into a rollover IRA, you have to deposit the full amount within the official time period—and the clock starts ticking on the date you receive the check.

A bigger problem is that 20% of the payout amount is automatically withheld to prepay tax when you get the payment check. That means if you're going to deposit the full amount, you'll have to tap another source—like your savings—to come up with the 20% that's

The answer will depend on:

- How much you have to transfer
- Your current tax rate
- Your age
- The time until you plan to withdraw

As with other Roth accounts, you must keep an account with transferred funds open for at least five years before you can take tax-free withdrawals. If you're not confident you'll wait that long, it's probably not smart to transfer your funds, pay the tax due and withdraw early, only to be faced with more taxes (and potentially a penalty).

One consideration if you are planning to transfer funds to a Roth IRA is that the tax on the entire amount will be due in the year the money is moved. That could be a very large tax bill if you've accumulated a substantial amount in your traditional IRA.

CONVERTING TO A ROTH

One way to take advantage of the tax-free income a Roth IRA provides is to convert your current IRA to a Roth. You'll owe the tax due on your earnings (and on your investment amount if you deducted your contributions), but no penalty. The catch is, your adjusted gross income can't be more than $100,000 in the year you make the transfer. The cap is the same whether you're single or married.

You'll probably want to get some expert advice on whether this strategy pays for you.

FUTURE CONSIDERATIONS

You can extend the tax-deferred life of your IRA by naming a living beneficiary rather than leaving it to your estate. That's because IRA withdrawals are based on life expectancy and an estate hasn't got one. So your account comes to a quick (and bad) end, with a tax bill to settle. It's an easy mistake to avoid.

---

being withheld. You'll get the 20% back—after you pay your taxes for the year, possibly as long as 15 or 16 months later.

Worse yet, if you can't come up with enough to cover the full lump sum payment, the amount that was withheld counts as a withdrawal, even though you never had the money. If you're not 59½ yet, you owe the tax, plus possibly a penalty for early withdrawal.

There is a way to avoid this problem: Have your employer transfer your pension payout to your rollover IRA directly, rather than sending you a check. That way, no tax is withheld. But if you want access to the cash during the 60 days, you're stuck.

2 INVEST WISELY

When you've moved the money from your old plan to your IRA, it's your responsibility to invest it to meet your long-term goals. One approach is to put the money into a money market mutual fund and move it gradually into the funds or individual investments you select. It's important, as part of the process, to diversify your portfolio.

3 CONSIDER ANOTHER ROLLOVER

If you take a new job where the employer offers a retirement savings plan that accepts rollovers from IRAs or other employer plans, you may choose to move your money into the plan. One thing to consider is the quality of the plan offerings, and whether you believe they will help you meet your objectives as well as investments you select on your own for your IRA. New rules allow you to move money from one type of plan—say a 403(b)—to another type—such as a 401(k). That increases your flexibility, and allows you to consolidate your retirement assets in one place.

4 PUT AWAY PENSION PAYOUTS

You can put all or part of your lump sum pension payout in a rollover IRA. If the payout is made in a series of partial lump sums over a period of less than ten years, you can put some or all of those payments into a rollover IRA too.

SEPs and SIMPLESs

Setting up a Simplified Employee Pension isn't exactly a piece of cake, but it can be a sweet addition to your retirement menu.

If you run a small business, a Simplified Employee Pension, or SEP, may offer the most effective way to put money away for retirement. That's because you can shelter a lot more than you can in an IRA and the rules, though they're involved, are a lot less stringent than for other qualified retirement plans, including Keoghs.

Because a SEP is a qualified plan, the amount you contribute each year for yourself and your employees can be deducted from your company's earnings, reducing your current taxes. The contribution cap is set for each year, as a dollar amount or percentage of earnings.

You also get flexibility with a SEP. You can change the amount of your contribution each year, skipping poor years and putting away the maximum in good ones. And if you end the plan, you can roll over the account into an IRA without penalty and keep earning money on a tax-deferred basis.

WHAT YOU CAN'T DO WITH SEPS

But there are a couple of restrictions on SEPs that don't apply to other retirement plans:

- **You must cover everyone who works for you**

- **You can't invest in insurance**

Neither of these by itself is reason to ignore the advantages of a SEP. And you don't have to file an annual report with the IRS the way you must with a Keogh.

EMPLOYEE PLANS

Since SEPs are actually specialized IRAs, sometimes referred to as SEP-IRAs, they're always set up and controlled by the person who benefits from them, even though they're funded exclusively by an employer.

That makes it easier if you're the employer: You don't have to pay someone to run a pension plan. It's also better if you're an employee: All the money in your SEP account is yours from the minute it's deposited. You don't have to wait to be vested, as you do with some other qualified plans.

Comparing SEP-IRAs

Small-company employees may be included in two different types of retirement savings plans. They are funded differently and have

SEP-IRA LIKE A PENSION, THE CONTRIBUTION COMES FROM YOUR EMPLOYER

Employer contributes up to 25% of your earnings or $41,000, whichever is less

You may be able to contribute

ALL ELIGIBLE EMPLOYEES MUST BE INCLUDED

EQUALITY'S THE RULE

If you have employees, you have to give them the same kind of SEP benefits you give yourself. For example, if you contribute 10% of your earnings to your SEP, you have to contribute 10% of their earnings to accounts in their names.

Anyone who is at least 21 years old, has worked for you for at least three of the last five years, and makes at least the annual minimum must be included. The only exceptions are nonresident aliens and certain union employees.

A SIMPLE PLAN

A simplified plan called a SIMPLE (Savings Incentive Match Plans for Employees) was introduced in 1997. Employees may contribute up to $9,000 in 2004, an amount that will increase to $10,000 in 2005. Employers must contribute either 2% for all eligible

and SIMPLEs

different rules for participating. But both make the contribution to an IRA in your name.

SIMPLE LIKE A 401(K), YOU MAKE THE BASIC CONTRIBUTION

You may contribute up to the annual salary cap

Employer must contribute, using one of two formulas

EMPLOYEES EARNING MORE THAN $5,000 MUST BE INCLUDED

SALARY REDUCTION SEP

Some older SEPs may have a **salary reduction plan**, also called an elective deferral, which allows employees as well as employers to contribute. If you're in such a plan you can defer up to the annual maximum that applies in similar retirement plans ($13,000 in 2004, increasing to $14,000 in 2005, and to $15,000 in 2006) in addition to what your employer puts in. However, no new SAR-SEPs, as these plans were known, can be established.

employees or match up to 3% of an employee's contribution.

While employees can contribute less to a SIMPLE than to a regular 401(k), the plans are also much less complicated to administer. In fact, they were designed to encourage more small companies to establish retirement plans.

SIMPLEs are set up so that contributions go into an IRA set up in each participant's name. That means everything in the account is **vested**, and belongs to you right from the start. Retirement savings don't have to be left behind if you change jobs.

However, SIMPLEs have stricter rules on tax-free transfers and early withdrawals than most other plans. Your account must be open for two years before you can move the money or take it out. If it hasn't been, you'll owe a 25% penalty on the amount transferred or withdrawn, rather than the usual 10% early withdrawal charge.

SIMPLE ALTERNATIVES

Employers may offer two other types of retirement savings plans, a SIMPLE 401(k) or a Safe Harbor 401(k).

Like a SIMPLE IRA, a SIMPLE 401(k) requires an employer to contribute to the plan for each qualifying employee—either 3% of what the employee contributes or 2% for all eligible employees. A major difference is that a SIMPLE 401(k) is a qualified plan, so the contributions are held in a qualified trust, not in a separate IRA for each participant.

From an employee's perspective a Safe Harbor 401(k) is more like a regular 401(k) than a SIMPLE, since the amount of salary that can be deferred is regular 401(k) amount—$13,000 in 2004 increasing annually to $15,000 in 2006. The difference is that, like a SIMPLE 401(k), employers must contribute to these plans. But in return they avoid having to do the annual nondiscrimination testing that can make offering retirement plans an administrative burden.

TIMING A SEP

Another appealing feature of SEPs is the timetable for setting up and contributing to the plan. Like an IRA, you can open a SEP and fund it when your income taxes are due.

In the long term, you'll benefit most if you contribute early in each tax year. But self-employed people often can't be sure how much they'll make or how much they'll be able to put away. Since there are penalties for investing too much, waiting until the end of the tax year makes it easier to get the contribution amount right.

Keogh Plans

A Keogh lets you invest for retirement while you're busy earning a living.

How to Qualify

If you're self-employed, earn money for work you do in addition to your regular job, or own a small business, you qualify to open a Keogh plan that lets you build up money for retirement by deferring taxes on the investments you make and the earnings they accumulate.

You can contribute a portion of your earnings from one or more of these categories, but no income from other sources. There's no requirement that these earnings be your only source of income or the Keogh be your only plan. In fact, you can be a fulltime employee covered by a defined benefits plan and still contribute to a Keogh if you earn money in a way that qualifies.

You may set up a Keogh if you:

Own your own business and file a Schedule C with your tax return

Work as a consultant

OPENING A KEOGH

To set up an Keogh, you need to file an IRS-approved plan. Banks and other financial institutions provide standardized plans, but you can have one specially designed by a lawyer or accountant who is a Keogh specialist. The advantage—some would say the necessity—of a specialized plan is the flexibility it provides for managing and investing your plan's assets.

KEOGHS FOR EMPLOYEES

If you have employees, and you have a Keogh plan for yourself, you must provide comparable benefits to the people who qualify to participate. In addition, if you contribute a certain percentage to one group of employees, you must treat all employees in that group alike.

The law says you must have a plan administrator—you can take the job

KEOGH or SEP?

If you qualify to set up a Keogh plan, you also qualify for a SEP—though you can't open both for the same earnings. Each has some advantages and some limitations.

For most people, especially those without employees, the debate comes down to two issues— the option to shelter more money through a Keogh versus the simplicity of a SEP. For employers, the ability to set the standards for participation can also be an important factor.

Advantages	Limitations
SEP	
● Simpler and cheaper to set up	● Employers with plan must cover everyone who works for them
● Easier to administer, both internally and for the IRS	
● Doesn't commit you to annual contributions	
KEOGH	
● Offers several ways to structure plan	● Can commit you to contributions even in poor years
● May let you shelter more money, sometimes much more	● Expensive to set up and administer
● Allows employers to establish criteria for employees to qualify for participation	● Complex tax-reporting requirements

THE MAN WITH THE PLAN
Keogh plans are named for Eugene Keogh, a U.S. Representative from Brooklyn, New York, who sponsored the legislation that established the plans. They went into effect in 1962.

Be self-employed doing something or selling something

Sit on a corporate board of directors

Be a partner in a business that files a Schedule K

Work as a freelancer

yourself if you want—and dictates how to compute contributions based on your income. There's no law that requires you to hire a Keogh specialist to handle your plan—but there probably ought to be.

HOW A KEOGH WORKS

A Keogh works like employer sponsored retirement plans in many ways. But like an IRA it is often set up to benefit just one person—you. Like other qualified plans, a Keogh lets you deduct pension contributions on your tax return and imposes a penalty if you withdraw funds before you're 59½.

When you reach 70½, you must set up a specific withdrawal schedule if you have retired. But if you continue to work and earn an income you may be able to continue to contribute and postpone withdrawals until April 1 of the year after you stop working unless you own more than 5% of the company. In that case, the 70½ rule applies even if you continue to work.

A Keogh allows you to borrow against the funds accumulated in your plan, with some restrictions. Neither of those advantages is available with an IRA or a SEP.

HOLD THE APPLAUSE

Keoghs are a boon to self-employed people who would otherwise have no way to shelter money for the future, and to employees of small businesses that wouldn't otherwise offer a retirement plan. But

being involved with a Keogh is complex. As an example, there are different Keogh regulations if you're self-employed, or if you're an employee of a company with a Keogh plan.

KEOGH CUSTOM TAILORING

CUSTOMIZE— IT MAY PAY OFF

Ask your lawyer or tax professional to recommend someone to set up your Keogh. Be prepared: A customized plan could cost several thousand dollars. But a plan that locks you into contributions you can't meet or options that limit what you can save costs more in the long run.

Once the account is set up—by December 31 of the first year you are going to take a tax deduction for your contribution—you can make annual or periodic additions to it as long as you don't put in more than the amount you're entitled to contribute in any given year. The deadline for depositing funds is the day your tax return is due, including any extensions you may get.

The same investment limitations that apply to IRAs apply to self-directed Keoghs, with an added prohibition on U.S. coins. But if your Keogh is a trust or custodial account, the money can be invested in anything at all—including wine.

Keogh Variety

Keoghs have several designs, plain and fancy, to appeal to a lot of different tastes.

While Keogh rules are notoriously complicated, the investment opportunities they provide have made them a staple of retirement planning. One major advantage is that you can choose the Keogh you want, from among several types of defined contribution options or a defined benefit plan. Another is that you can customize a plan that suits you, whether you're its only beneficiary or you have other employees.

Defined contribution plans, which are available in three different versions, are classic Keoghs. They work just like corporate defined contribution retirement plans. You put money into the plan, and the amount you have at retirement depends chiefly on how well your investments do.

Defined benefit plans guarantee a specific payout but may require large contributions. They are not for everyone. But they can be ideal for people within 15 years or so of retirement who are making lots of money and don't mind the expense of sheltering it this way.

JUST DESSERTS

MAKE YOUR OWN

DIET SPECIAL

CHOOSE YOUR FLAVORS

DOUBLE SCOOPS

PROFIT-SHARING DEFINED CONTRIBUTION PLANS are the least complicated, and the most popular, Keoghs.

They let you decide each year whether to participate and how much to put away.

You can contribute up to 25% of earnings, or $41,000, whichever is less.

Those limits, and others, may increase in the future.

MONEY PURCHASE DEFINED CONTRIBUTION PLANS let you put away up to 25% of all eligible employees' earnings. Each employee can receive up to a maximum of $41,000.

You must specify the percentage of earnings when you set up the plan, and you must contribute that percentage each year. The minimum you can choose is 3%. If you don't put in enough, you'll owe a penalty of up to 100% of the amount you owed but didn't contribute.

PAIRED PLANS, combining aspects of profit-sharing and money purchase plans, were once popular because they allowed you to put away more money when the contribution cap for money purchase was higher than for profit sharing.

And while they required an annual contribution, they allowed you to set the required percentage low enough—say 10%—to meet comfortably each year.

However, many employers have converted these plans to straight profit sharing.

MAKING THE CONTRIBUTION

The maximum you can add to a Keogh each year is a fixed percentage of earnings or a maximum dollar amount, to a limit determined by the particular plan you're using, as described below. For 2003, the maximum contribution ranges from 25% to 100%, with all three versions of defined contribution plans capped at $40,000. IRS Publication 560 has all the details, or you can work with a retirement plan specialist.

In most cases, you'll end up making your contribution after the end of your fiscal year, when you know for certain what your earnings are. That's especially true if you're self-employed or if your income is unpredictable, and you can't be sure what your balance sheet will show.

DEFINED BENEFIT
PLANS guarantee a specific annual payout after you retire or reach age 65.

To fund the plan so that it produces the payout you choose (and incidentally to save yourself a lot of current tax), you may be able to contribute up to 100% of your annual earnings.

Figuring out what you must pay in each year is extremely complicated. The law requires that an actuary review your plan annually to determine what you have to put in to meet your projected payout. You must submit a copy of that report with your tax return.

KEOGH TRUSTS

If you want to diversify your Keogh investments without having to watch several different plans, you can set up a self-directed Keogh trust, make all your contributions to the trust, and invest the holdings as you choose. While setting up a trust can be costly and time-consuming, it does more than just save paperwork over time. With a trust, you can make more types of investments and shift your asset allocation among investments more easily.

Perhaps most important, a trust simplifies the withdrawal process when the time comes to start taking your money out, since unlike IRAs, you must withdraw the correct amount from each Keogh account separately.

KEEPING THE IRS UP TO DATE

Keoghs can be a recordkeeping nightmare. You may have to file an annual report with the IRS, using form 5500EZ if you're self-employed, or several schedules with form 5500 if you have employees. Even if you have to gather the records yourself, it's probably worth having an accountant or Keogh expert fill out the forms for you.

IRS FORM 5500-C

IRS FORM 5500EZ

IRS FORM 5500-R

ELASTIC PLANS

If you have a Keogh, you can roll a pension payout from another job into it, instead of into an IRA, which may give you more flexibility when you start withdrawing from your retirement plans.

Or, if your self-employment income dries up and you can't keep up with a Keogh plan, you can call it quits and roll the money over into an IRA. You're out the money you spent to set your plan up, and might have to pay some penalties. But because a Keogh is a qualified retirement plan, you don't have to take a distribution and pay tax on it.

IRA Withdrawals

You have to be old enough to take money out of your IRA, but you don't have to retire first.

The first things you have to know about withdrawing from your tax-deferred retirement investments are the magic numbers. One is the otherwise unmagical 59½. That's the point at which you can begin to collect without paying a penalty.

Being eligible at 59½ doesn't mean you must start collecting then: You can wait until you actually retire—at 62 or 65 or 68—or until you're ready to add a source of income to your budget.

The only restriction is that you *must* begin withdrawing from a traditional IRA after you reach age 70½. In fact, you must set up a plan for getting all the money out of your accounts and into your pockets (and the taxes you owe into Uncle Sam's pockets).

If you have a Roth IRA, though, you don't have to set up a plan, or make withdrawals at all, for that matter, if you don't need the money. On the other hand, since Roth withdrawals are tax free, it may make more sense to use that income than income from taxable investments.

59½ [60–70] 70½

Since insurance company actuarial tables consider you already 60 when you reach 59½, and still 70 until you're 70½, Congress used those ages to frame the withdrawal period from retirement accounts.

WHEN WITHDRAWALS ARE A MUST

Since an IRA is a retirement account, with the tax-deferral advantage, the IRS doesn't want it to be a way to build the estate you're planning to leave your heirs. So after you reach age 70½, the law says you must start spending what you've saved—whether you need the money or not. But if there are assets left in your account when you die, the person or people you name as beneficiaries can spread the withdrawals over their lifetimes, potentially extending the benefits for many years.

WHAT YOU HAVE TO TAKE

You figure the amount you must withdraw starting at age 70½ by dividing the value of your IRA on December 31 of the previous year by your life expectancy. For example, if your account is worth $200,000 and your life expectancy is 27.4 years—as it is when you're 70—you must take a minimum of $7,299 ($200,000 ÷ 27.4 = $7,299.27, or $7,299) in that year.

Everyone uses the same life expectancy table, which you can find in IRS Publication 590, "Individual Retirement Arrangements (IRAs)." The only exception is that if you name your spouse as beneficiary and he or she is more than ten years younger than you are. Then you can use a different table, which produces a longer life expectancy and a smaller required withdrawal amount.

If you don't withdraw, or you take less than you should, you are vulnerable to a 50% penalty on the amount you should have withdrawn.

THE TAX BITE

The tax you owe on your traditional IRA withdrawals is figured at your regular tax rate. That's why some experts advise keeping investments you expect to grow in value, like higher-risk stocks and mutual funds, in regular taxable accounts. You don't owe tax on their increasing value until you sell, and then you pay at the lower capital gains rate.

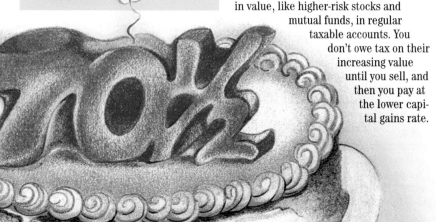

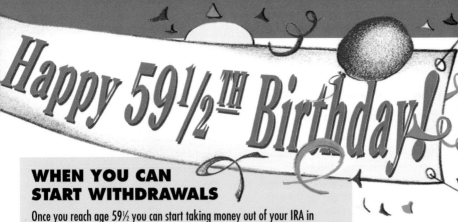

Happy 59½TH Birthday!

WHEN YOU CAN START WITHDRAWALS

Once you reach age 59½ you can start taking money out of your IRA in any amount you want. You'll owe tax on the amount you withdraw from a traditional account, but you can spend it any way you like. With a Roth, there's no tax at all.

TAKING IT EARLY

Since there are exceptions to the rule against early withdrawals from your IRA, the government has done you—and itself—a favor. It won't cost you a 10% penalty if you take money out of your IRAs to pay education expenses, put money down on your first home or support your family while you're disabled.

But you will owe taxes at your regular rate, giving the government added revenue. For example, a couple in their 40s who withdraw $100,000 from retirement accounts to pay their child's college expenses could owe more than 40% of it in federal and state income taxes.

Before you make that choice, you might compare what it costs to take a home equity loan, with its tax-deductible interest, with the tax bill that comes with taking money out of your IRA. It may turn out that borrowing costs less. Another way to borrow is to tap your qualified retirement plans, including 401(k)s or similar accounts. While the amount you can borrow may be limited, the interest you pay goes back into your account, helping to offset loss of earnings.

When It's Safe to Withdraw

10% PENALTY FOR EARLY WITHDRAWAL	NO PENALTY FOR WITHDRAWALS BETWEEN AGES 59½ TO 70½	50% PENALTY FOR LATE WITHDRAWAL

| 50 | 59½ | 70½ | 80 |

EARLY WITHDRAWAL WITHOUT PENALTY

There is one way to get access to the money in your IRAs before you're 59½ and avoid the penalty. That's to **annuitize** your distribution. It means you establish a withdrawal plan that pays you, each year, a fixed amount of the money in your IRA, based on your life expectancy. The chief restriction is that the plan must cover at least five years or all the years left until you reach 59½, whichever is longer. Annuitization does have drawbacks, though. If what you really need is a large amount of money, you probably won't get it this way unless you're close to 59½. And you're using money that was intended for your retirement, so you're depleting, not adding, to your savings.

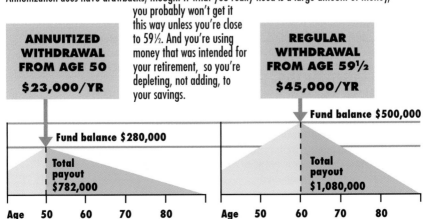

ANNUITIZED WITHDRAWAL FROM AGE 50

$23,000/YR

REGULAR WITHDRAWAL FROM AGE 59½

$45,000/YR

Fund balance $500,000

Fund balance $280,000

Total payout $782,000

Total payout $1,080,000

Age 50 60 70 80   Age 50 60 70 80

Taking Money Out

Using up the assets in your traditional IRA can require some fancy footwork.

When you're ready to start taking money out of your traditional IRAs, you need a strategy to meet the legal withdrawal requirements while getting the best return you can. You must take out at least the required minimum, and may take more if you need the money for living expenses. But you also want your accounts to continue to grow, ensuring that you'll have a source of income for as many years as you need it.

STRATEGIC PLANNING

If you've accumulated a substantial IRA with regular contributions or have transferred other retirement plan payouts into a rollover IRA, you'll want to look at the big picture before planning your withdrawals. One issue is deciding which accounts to draw on first, and another is selecting the way the money moves from the IRA into your hands.

If your IRA investment is in mutual funds, for example, you can set up a regular—usually monthly—distribution. Similarly, if you invest in an immediate annuity, you can **annuitize**, which means creating an income stream of monthly payments. It makes sense to investigate the various payment possibilities, including the fees that might apply. When you decide which approach is best for you, you can put your plan into action and start collecting.

Here's some good news: There's no penalty for taking too much out of your accounts too quickly. And, after your death, a beneficiary can generally withdraw from your account over his or her own life expectancy.

HOW LONG WILL YOU LIVE?

The funny thing about life expectancy is that the longer you live, the longer you can expect to live. According to the IRS, life expectancy at birth is 82.4. But at 82, life expectancy is 91. At 91, it's 96. And when you reach 96, you can expect to live until you're 100.

1

ADD UP YOUR IRAs
Withdrawals are based on the total value of all your accounts.

SETTING THE AMOUNT

Between ages 59½ and 70½, you may take as much or as little as you wish from your IRA each year without penalty. After you reach 70½, you must take at least the required minimum each year. You find that amount by dividing your account value by a **uniform withdrawal factor** based on your life expectancy.

You can take the entire withdrawal from just one IRA at a time, even if you have several. One advantage is that you can postpone withdrawing from accounts that are growing at a faster rate. Another is simplified bookkeeping.

2

FIGURE YOUR WITHDRAWAL AMOUNT
You don't want your account to provide too little money or run out too quickly.

GETTING THE RIGHT NUMBERS

If you have $250,000 in your IRA, and you have a life expectancy of 20.3 years, you need to withdraw $12,315.27. You can use the formula below for figuring out the size of the withdrawal you have to make:

$$\frac{\text{Account balance}}{\text{Uniform withdrawal factor}} = \frac{\text{Minimum annual withdrawal}}{}$$

for example

$$\frac{\$250,000}{20.3} = \$12,315.27$$

INDIVIDUAL PLANS

DOING THE MATH

The IRS provides a **uniform withdrawal factor**, formerly known as a life expectancy table, to help you determine your **minimum required distribution (MRD)**, or the annual amount you must withdraw each year after you turn 70½. This simplified method introduced in 2001 not only makes figuring the amount easier, but usually decreases the amount you must withdraw each year.

Smaller required withdrawals reduce the potential problem of outliving your assets simply by outliving your life expectancy. For more information, get a

IRS PUB 590

You can get Publication 590 and other tax information on the IRS website at www.irs.gov or by calling:

1-800-TAX-FORM

copy of IRS Publication 590. You may also want to consult your tax adviser or a retirement planning specialist.

Calculating your MRD is easy. Simply divide the value of your IRA by your uniform withdrawal factor, which is determined by your age.

Table III (Uniform Lifetime) (For Use by Owners)	
Age	Distribution Period
70	27.4
71	26.5
72	25.6
73	24.7
74	23.8
75	22.9
76	22.0
77	21.2
78	20.3
79	19.5

MINIMUM REQUIRED DISTRIBUTION FOR A $100,000 IRA

Age	Uniform Withdrawal Factor
70	27.4

$$\frac{\$100,000}{27.4} = \$3,650 \text{ MRD}$$

Age	Uniform Withdrawal Factor
75	22.9

$$\frac{\$100,000}{22.9} = \$4,367 \text{ MRD}$$

3

AVOID TAX PENALTIES

You'll owe extra tax for withdrawing too little.

GETTING THE NUMBERS WRONG

If you miscalculate the amount you must withdraw and take too little, you'll get socked with a 50% penalty on the additional amount you should have taken and didn't. That's true even if it was an honest mistake—unless you can prove to the IRS that you were completely befuddled.

If you take large withdrawals, of course, you pay more tax than you might have otherwise, and you'll deplete your account faster. But there aren't penalties for that.

4

IRA WITHDRAWAL
☐ Bonds
☐ Stocks
☐ CD
☐ Money Mkt.

DECIDE ON A SOURCE

You have to decide which investments to sell or withdraw from.

FINDING THE CASH

Figuring out how much you must withdraw each year is only part of your task. You also have to decide how to get at it. Since wise investment strategy suggests you diversify your retirement accounts in several asset classes, you probably won't have the exact withdrawal amount just sitting in a savings account.

You could sell stocks, but what if the market is down? You might have to pay a penalty to take money out of a CD. A better option may be to open a mutual fund or bank money market account to collect dividends, interest payments, and redemptions.

Social Security

Social Security is an American institution—now. But it was controversial at the start.

Social Security is a safety net, designed to provide a financial foundation for retired and disabled workers and their families. People without other sources of income get by entirely on their Social Security benefits. But for many Americans, the monthly payment supplies just a part of their retirement budget.

Before Social Security, veterans—disabled ones in particular—got pensions. And in the early 20th century, payments to civilian government workers and to needy widows and orphans grew out of the notion that social welfare was a government responsibility. But public opinion was widely split, not only on providing benefits, but on who deserved support.

RELIEF FOR DEPRESSION

President Roosevelt introduced the **Social Security Act** in 1935 as part of his New Deal, a controversial recovery plan designed to cope with the devastating aftermath of the Great Depression and its particularly chilling effect on the financial situation of the elderly and the unemployed.

Today, benefits for retired and disabled workers and their survivors have evolved into the most elaborate and most popular social program in the U.S. Unemployment compensation is also firmly in place. But the other two elements of Roosevelt's original program—public assistance, or welfare, and universal health care insurance—remain controversial.

A COMPULSORY PLAN

Since other countries had tried voluntary retirement income plans without success, Congress decided that everybody who was going to be eligible for benefits had to participate by contributing part of their earnings. To simplify the collection process, they originated the idea of **withholding** and passed the Federal Insurance Contribution Act (FICA) which:

- **Authorized employers to deduct workers' contribution amounts directly from their salaries**

- **Made employers responsible for forwarding the FICA taxes to the Internal Revenue Service (IRS)**

WHERE IT BEGAN

Americans didn't invent the idea of Social Security, although there was a precedent in the pensions paid to Union veterans of the Civil War. In 1889, **Chancellor Otto von Bismarck** made old age insurance compulsory in Germany, requiring that working people, their employers, and the government all contribute to a program that would provide financial support after retirement. Retired worker programs were widespread in Europe by the 1920s.

EMPLOYER CONTRIBUTIONS

The Social Security system wouldn't have enough money to operate if it ran on employee contributions alone, no matter how big a bite your share seems to take out of your paycheck. So employers are required to pay taxes on the wages they pay their workers equal to the amount the employee pays. That's true no matter how few or how many employees there are.

If you're self-employed, you pay both shares, or twice the amount you would pay if you worked for someone else. You can deduct half of your total payment (the equivalent of the employer's share) on your income tax return. And it doesn't reduce what you can contribute to a SEP-IRA, money purchase, or profit sharing retirement plan.

ALMOST ALL INCLUSIVE

Originally, Social Security included only commercial and industrial employees, but over the years it's been expanded to cover more than 90% of the work force. Several groups of workers don't participate, including some state and local government employees and railroad workers (who have their own retirement plans), and some members of the clergy who don't participate for religious reasons.

People who don't work aren't part of the system either, although they may qualify for benefits as the spouse, child or dependent of someone who has participated in the system.

DOING THE JOB

Social Security insures the financial security of a large—and growing—segment of the population. More than 90% of all households that include someone over 65 get benefits. It provides the main source of income for 64% of the households receiving retirement benefits. And it has achieved one of its primary goals, dramatically reducing poverty rates among people over 65. Without their Social Security income, more than half of the elderly population would be poor according to government standards. But because of the benefits, only 8% fall into that category.

A WIDE NET

There are very few people eligible for Social Security benefits who aren't collecting them. If you move frequently or don't have a permanent address, there's sometimes a delay in getting your payment. But you can collect Social Security almost anywhere in the world—except in jail.

The one group of people who may not be collecting, but should be, are those over 65 who are still working full time. Social Security rules let you collect your full benefit no matter how many hours you work or how much you earn once you reach 65. It doesn't make sense to delay collecting past age 70, because the basic benefit you're entitled to then is the highest it will be.

GET IN TOUCH

You can get recorded information about Social Security coverage 24 hours a day by calling 800-772-1213, and you can speak to a representative if you call between 7 a.m. and 7 p.m. on business days. Or you can visit the Social Security website at www.ssa.gov

Changing for the Better

A big part of the system's strength has been its flexibility.

Signing the legislation was only the first step in creating the enormous institution that Social Security has become. Today, it's a comprehensive program that administers retirement, survivor and disability benefits, plus a Supplemental Security Program (SSI) for the low-income elderly and disabled people.

Growing Pains

The system has been changing, almost since the day it began. Things that once seemed impossible, like getting coverage if you were self-employed, or having to pay taxes on your benefits, are now the norm.

1939 In 1939, supplemental benefits for spouses and children were added to the payment a retired worker received. Payments began in 1940.

1951 In 1951, coverage was extended to include self-employed workers, as well as others who had not been eligible before, including farmers, domestic workers and entrepreneurs.

We've got your number

Identifying the people putting money into the Social Security system—and expecting to get money back—posed another challenge. Names and addresses wouldn't work: People change their names, and they move. How could the government be sure they had the right Charles Smith or Maria Rodriguez? Or that River Road was in Grandview, Ohio, not Grand View, New York?

The solution was assigning everyone a nine-digit number that would last a lifetime, through name changes, job changes, and new addresses. And the system could identify 999,999,999 people without ever having to use the same number twice.

The first three digits indicate the state where you applied for a card. The number changes as more cards are issued in that state.

The second group of digits doesn't have a particular meaning—though it is related to the order in which cards are issued in a region.

The last four digits are assigned in numerical order, for example 7091, 7092, 7093, and so on. One exception: twins, triplets, or other multiple siblings don't get numbers in order.

EXPLODING USES

Once, you needed a Social Security number to open a Social Security account and keep track of your contributions. Now, you need one for almost anything you want to do:

- **Get a job**
- **File income tax returns**
- **Enroll as a student**
- **Open a bank, brokerage or mutual fund account**
- **Get a passport or a driver's license**
- **Ask for an insurance payment**
- **Apply for a loan**
- **Request your credit rating**

1957 In 1957, members of the armed forces were covered.

1972 In 1972, benefit increases were linked, or indexed, to inflation, to increase as the cost of living increased.

1966 In 1966, witholding was increased to pay for Medicare insurance benefits.

1984 In 1984, federal workers and employees of non-profit organizations were covered by Social Security.

1995 In 1995, the SSA became an independent agency by act of Congress. President Clinton signed the bill 59 years and one day after FDR signed the original Act.

BY THE NUMBERS

The IRS requires everyone to have a Social Security number if he or she is going to be claimed as a dependent on a tax return. In fact, in many states, babies are given a number when their births are registered.

Your number—one of the 400 million that's been assigned so far—can be changed, usually if your records have been confused with someone else's who has the same name and birthdate, or if someone has used your number illegally.

CHANGING YOUR NAME

If you change your name when you get married or divorced, or if you change it legally for any other reason, you can file form SS-5 and have the change made on your Social Security account. You'll have to provide your marriage license, divorce decree, or other legal proof. Your Social Security number doesn't change, though, and your credits are intact.

THREE TYPES OF CARDS

People talk about Social Security cards as if they were all alike, but there are actually several types. Basic cards go to citizens and people living permanently in the U.S. You need the card—or at least the number—to get a job, collect benefits, and, increasingly, as a universal ID number.

People who are in the country legally, but for a limited time, may get Social Security cards to open bank accounts, for example, or enroll in college. Their cards are stamped *Not Eligible For Employment,* and they're not eligible for benefits. In 1992, a third type was added, stamped *Valid For Work Only With INS* (Immigration and Naturalization Service) *Authorization.*

Those cards permit legal immigrants to get jobs and qualify for benefits.

Legally, it's up to a potential employer to be sure that anyone who's hired to work is eligible—and checking for a valid Social Security card is the primary method.

JUST THE BEGINNING

Ida Fuller, of Ludlow, VT, got a check for $22.54 in January, 1940—the first monthly benefit that Social Security paid. But that was only the beginning. Fuller lived to be 99, and the $20 she paid in withholding tax was repaid a thousand times in the three decades she collected.

Benefit Ins and Outs

One of every six Americans—about 49 million people—gets Social Security benefits.

THE MONEY GOING IN:

6.2% OF 154 MILLION PAYCHECKS FOR SOCIAL SECURITY

1.45% FOR MEDICARE

(PLUS EQUAL AMOUNTS FROM EMPLOYER)

The 6.2% that's withheld is used to make current Social Security payments and to build the reserve that will be needed to meet future needs. It's deposited into two Social Security Trust Funds, one for retirement benefits and the other for disability payments. The 1.45% withheld for Medicare goes into trust funds set up to pay for medical care.

RETIREMENT TRUST FUND

The core of the Social Security program is a guaranteed monthly income designed to insure a basic level of financial support for retired or disabled people, their families, and their survivors. It's funded by money withheld from your paycheck, and the paychecks of 154 million other working Americans.

SETTING YOUR CONTRIBUTION

The amount you owe for retirement, survivor, and disability insurance is 6.2% of your earned income (including salary, tips, commissions and bonuses) up to a specific limit that's adjusted each year to reflect increases in the cost of living. For 2004, the income limit is $87,900, in comparison to $84,900 in 2002 and $80,400 in 2001.

If you earn less than the limit, 6.2% of your gross, or pre-tax, earnings is withheld from each paycheck throughout the year. If you earn more, the deduction disappears when you've paid the full amount for the year.

Your income from pensions, investments (including annuities), capital gains, sick pay, unemployment insurance or alimony isn't considered earned, so it escapes the long arm of withholding.

MEDICARE COSTS MORE

There's more, though. An additional 1.45% is withheld to fund Medicare benefits for people over 65. There's been no cap on your Medicare obligation, which means that 1.45% of whatever you earn is withheld throughout the year.

WHERE'S THE LIMIT

There's an annual cap for retirement contributions, but none for Medicare.	6.2% deduction stops when cap is reached	1.45% deduction never stops
Salary	for example **SS deduction**	for example **Medicare deduction**
$ 20,000	$ 1,240	$ 290
$ 45,000	$ 2,790	$ 652.50
$87,900	$ 5,449.80 CAP	$1,274.55
$ 110,000	$ 5,449.80	$1,595

WITHHOLDING TOO MUCH

If you have more than one job, or if you work on your own in addition to holding a job, you may have too much Social Security withheld. For example,

- If you earned $89,000 in 2004 at your regular job, $5,449.80, the maximum amount, was withheld

- If you earned another $15,000 working nights and weekends, your employer withheld $930 (or 6.2% of $15,000)

- That made your total withholding $6,379.80, or $930 too much

WHAT'S INCOME—TO THE SSA

What counts	What doesn't count
Wages	Most pension income
Tips	Capital gains
Commissions	Sick pay
Self-employment income	Unemployment
	Alimony
	Investment income (including annuities)

Both employers must withhold at the regular rate, as if each of them were your only employer—even if they know you're working two jobs. The same thing happens if you're self-employed. You owe Social Security tax on what you earn even if you have the maximum withheld at another job.

You don't actually end up overpaying. The excess is credited toward the income tax you owe when you pay your taxes. But you are out the money in the meantime.

The only exception occurs when you have too much withheld by one employer, which can happen if you get back pay or a bonus. Then it's your employer's job to repay the extra withholding directly to you.

DISABILITY TRUST FUND   MEDICARE TRUST FUND

THE MONEY GOING OUT:

MORE THAN $1.3 BILLION A DAY, TO 47 MILLION PEOPLE

TREASURY BONDS

The money in the various trust funds is invested in U.S. Treasury bonds, safely earning interest, while the government uses it to keep its operations running. So far, the system has worked, and current obligations are regularly met.

BENEFIT PAYMENTS

Social Security pays out more than $1 billion a day. The average retirement payment is $926 a month. The average disability check is $866.

About 47 million people will receive benefits in 2004: retired workers and their dependents, survivors, and disabled workers and their families. Among the beneficiaries, about 42% were men and 58% were women.

WHAT THE FUTURE HOLDS

Nobody can say for sure what will happen to Social Security during the 21st century. But its history has been evolutionary from the start, and that's likely to continue. Changes that caused major uproars when they were enacted—like taxing retirement benefits—have become the norm. The only thing that seems impossible is abandoning the system altogether.

But eventually the people collecting benefits will outnumber the people putting money into the system. That may mean that wealthy retired people will get less than they expected, or nothing at all. Or all benefits may be taxed. Or cost-of-living increases might be smaller.

Social Security Up Close

Representatives at your local Social Security office provide advice and assistance face-to-face.

Much of the time, you deal with the Social Security Administration from a distance, using the phone or website to get information, open an account, or even apply for benefits. But sooner or later, you'll probably visit your local Social Security office, one of 1,300 in the country. The offices can be quite different physically, but they're all equipped to handle the same things, helping you to join the system or take advantage of the benefits it provides. In particular, they can provide up-to-date estimates of what your benefits would be if you chose different options, like retiring early, or getting benefits as a survivor instead of based on your own work history.

Over 6 million new numbers are issued annually, making the 2000 total about 400 million

It takes just a week to get a card if you apply in person

OPENING A SOCIAL SECURITY ACCOUNT

If you got a Social Security number when you were young, your account is open even if you've never worked. But if you don't have a number, you don't have an account. Getting one is relatively simple, though. You fill out form SS-5 which you can get at your local Social Security office and submit it along with evidence to prove your age, identity, and citizenship. You need your birth certificate (or a hospital record or baptismal certificate if you don't have one), plus one other piece of identification, like a passport, driver's license, or school record. The SS-5 application includes a list of the documents Social Security will accept. Parents opening accounts for their children must also prove their own identity and parenthood or guardianship.

If you're over 18, you must appear in person to open your account. If you're younger, you can do the whole thing by mail, but you may not want to. You have to provide Social Security with original copies of your birth certificate and other documents, and you probably don't want to risk having them lost or misplaced.

Don't worry if the nearest office is too far for you to travel to. Social Security representatives visit contact stations in rural areas on a regular schedule. And, if you're unable to get to the office because you're too ill or infirm, and can't get your case resolved over the telephone, they will come to your home.

IDENTIFYING YOURSELF

U.S. citizens born in hospitals within the country's boundaries usually have no trouble providing a birth certificate. But if you were born outside the U.S., you may have to produce extra identification, even if your parents are U.S. citizens.

If you're a naturalized citizen you'll need your citizenship papers as well as a birth record. And if you're not a citizen, you'll need either a birth certificate or passport and documents from the Immigration and Naturalization Service.

USING A REPRESENTATIVE

Most people deal with Social Security directly, but it is legal to pay someone to represent you in filing claims, appealing decisions, or even collecting your benefits. You must file several forms and name your representative. And that person must get written approval from Social Security to charge you a fee. The usual limit is 25% of past-due benefits paid, plus out-of-pocket expenses.

Approximately 156 million workers are fully insured for retirement and disability benefits

More than 4 million new benefits awards were made in 2000—nearly half to retired workers

SUPPLEMENTAL SECURITY INCOME

If you don't qualify for Social Security, or if your benefits are very small, you may be eligible for Supplemental Security Income (SSI). Unlike other Social Security benefits, these are paid with funds from the regular government budget, not with payroll taxes.

In 2004, more than six million needy aged, blind or disabled people got SSI benefits. Benefit limits for individuals and married couples are set each year.

To be eligible, you can't have more than $2,000 in assets if you're single and $3,000 if you're a couple. That doesn't include your home or car, but it does include savings and other investments. Your income also must be

To qualify for SSI you must be a U.S. citizen and fit one of these categories:

- 65 or older
- Blind
- Disabled

below a specific level, although the amount varies depending on whether or not you work and the state where you live.

The Social Security Administration runs the program and is the best source for information about the benefits it provides.

Got You Covered

It pays to be one of the Social Security crowd.

You have to qualify for Social Security benefits, but it's not hard to do. If you work for a total of ten years—even if you do it a few months at a time, and never earn more than the minimum amount—you'll be entitled to Social Security benefits when you retire. You qualify for Medicare the same way.

People who've worked early in their lives and then left the work force, like women raising families, can return to work after a long break and still accumulate enough credits to qualify for the various programs. Though the dollar amount of a late qualifier's benefit is usually smaller than someone's who has worked all along, the security of knowing you have coverage is the same.

Checking the Details

Your Social Security Statement reports:

The **maximum earnings** that were subject to Social Security tax each year.

Your **earnings that were taxed** for Social Security each year since you started working.

The **monthly benefit you'd receive** if you started collecting at 62, at your full retirement age, or if you waited until you were 70 to collect.

Your Social Security Earnings

Years	Social Security			Estimated Taxes You Paid	Maximum Taxable Earnings	Med... Re... Ea...
	Maximum Taxable Earnings	Your Reported Earnings				
1989	48,000	34,670		2,101	48,000	3...
1990	51,300	51,300		3,180	51,300	5
1991	53,400	53,400		3,310	125,000	5
1992	55,500	38,267		2,372	130,200	3
1993	57,600	57,600		3,571	135,000	1
1994	60,600	60,600		3,757	No Limit	...
1995	61,200	61,200		3,794	No Limit	
1996	62,700	62,700		3,887	No Limit	
1997	65,400	65,400		4,054	No Limit	
1998	68,400	68,400		4,240	No Limit	
1999	72,600	72,600		4,501	No Limit	
2000	76,200	76,200		4,724	No Limit	
2001	80,400	80,400		4,984	No Limit	

Total estimated Social Security taxed paid $ 51,323

Retirement

If you retire at 62, your monthly benefit in today's dollars will be about. . . . . **$ 975**

The earliest age at which you can receive an unreduced retirement benefit is 65 and 10 months. We call this your full retirement age. If you wait until that age to receive benefits, your monthly benefit in today's dollars will be about . . . . **$ 1,325**

If you wait until you are 70 to receive benefits, your monthly benefit in today's dollars will be about . . . . **$ 1,790**

SOCIAL SECURITY
40 CREDITS
QUALIFIED

PUTTING IN YOUR TIME

Social Security is based on a system of **credits** you earn while you're working. To receive retirement benefits, you need to accumulate 40 credits. In 2004, you earned one credit for each $900 you made. But you earn only four credits a year, no matter how much you make. For example, a college student who earned $3,600 painting houses during the summer accumulated four credits. So did a bond trader who earned 100 times that amount.

2004 INCOME	CREDITS EARNED
$ 0	0
$ 900	1
$ 3,600	4

TRACKING YOUR RECORD

Each year the Social Security Administration (SSA) sends each participant age 25 and older a personal Social Security Statement. It reports what you've contributed over your working life and estimates the monthly benefit amounts that you'll qualify for at retirement or if you're disabled. The report should arrive about three months before your birthday. If it doesn't, you can follow up by calling the SSA at 800-772-1213 or clicking on Social Security Statement on the website (www. ssa.gov).

The SSA encourages you to check the form against your own work records to be sure the details are right. If they're wrong—and they sometimes are—you can submit copies of your W-2 withholding statements and your tax returns to get them corrected. The more quickly you realize there's a problem, the easier it will be to resolve.

Estimated
Taxes
You Paid

502
743
836
554
1,957
1,056
1,419
1,123

The **tax you paid each year** shows the amount for retirement, survivor and disability insurance. The amount for Medicare is recorded separately. If you started working for the **federal government** before 1984, and aren't covered by Social Security, the form will show you the tax you paid for Medicare coverage.

Survivors

Here is an estimate of the benefits your family could receive if you had enough credits to be insured, they qualified for benefits, and you died this year:

Your child could receive a monthly benefit of about. . | $ 805

If your child and your surviving spouse who is caring for your child both qualify, they could each receive a monthly benefit of about. . . . . | $ 805

When your surviving spouse reaches full retirement age, he or she could receive a monthly benefit of about. . . | $ 1,075

The **amount your survivors would be paid** if you died during the year the estimate was made.

The **disability benefit you and your family would get** every month if you were not able to work and qualified for benefits.

Disability

If you were disabled, had enough credits, and met the other requirements for disability benefits, here is an estimate of the benefits you could receive right now:

Your monthly benefit would be about. . . . . | $ 1,060

You and your eligible family members could receive up to a monthly total of about. . . . . | $ 1,590

These estimates may be ~~~
compensation ~~~

The minimum dollar amount per credit is increased every year to reflect changes in the cost of living, just as the maximum income on which you pay Social Security taxes is. But once you hit 40 credits, you're set. Working longer may mean your benefit is larger, but you don't need more credits.

RAPID INCREASES

The amount of your salary that gets taxed for Social Security has increased dramatically in recent years. In its first 35 years, the SSA raised the ceiling only five times,

from $3,000 in 1937 to $7,800 in 1972. Since then, when the amount that's taxable was indexed to inflation, it has gone up every year, with the biggest percentage jump between 1980 and 1981, from $25,900 to $29,700, a whopping 14.7% increase.

$87,900

$72,600

$7,800

$3,000   TAXABLE CEILING

1937   1972   1999 2004

Figuring What You Get

Figuring out how much you'll get is a lot harder than qualifying.

Chances are you'll take the SSA's word for the size of your benefit. Figuring it out is complicated, because your career-long earnings must be adjusted to their approximate current value to determine the wage base on which your benefit is figured. The $5,000 you made in 1969, for instance, isn't averaged in as $5,000.

WHAT COUNTS

Unlike most pensions, which are based on what you're earning at the end of your career, Social Security counts what you've earned during most of your working life, specifically five years fewer than the number of credits you need to qualify. So, if you were born after 1928 and need 40 credits to be eligible for benefits, your 35 highest paying years are the ones that count in figuring what you will receive.

Like other pensions, though, the more you've earned, the more you get. If you've paid the maximum tax each year and wait until you reach full retirement age to start collecting, you'll get the largest benefit Social Security gives.

UNDERSTANDING THE FORMULA

The SSA figures your benefit, or **primary insurance amount (PIA)**, like this:

What the SSA does	For example
First, they index your earnings up to age 60 to their approximate current value. (Earnings after 60 are counted as they are.)	If the average earnings in 2001 were about five times greater than in 1971, the $10,000 you earned then would be multiplied by five and adjusted to $50,000. The adjustment factor is smaller for more recent years.
Next, they total your earnings for your highest 35 years and divide by 420 (the months in 35 years) to find your **average indexed monthly earnings (AIME).**	If your adjusted earnings were $50,000 a year for 30 years, you'd multiply the two and divide by 420—since all 35 years count even if you weren't working: $1,500,000 ÷ 420 = $3,571
Finally, they compute your basic benefit rate by figuring 90% of the first $561, 32% of the next $2,820, and 15% of the balance and adding the results. The dollar amounts, or **bend points**, for each bracket are adjusted every year.	With an AIME of $3,571, your basic rate, or primary insurance amount, would be $1,435.80 (rounded to the next lower dime) 90% of $561 = $ 504.90 32% of $2,820 = $ 902.40 15% of $190 = $ 28.50 $ 1,435.80 PIA

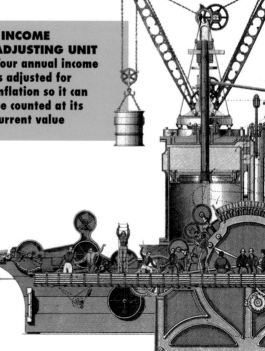

2 INCOME ADJUSTING UNIT
Your annual income is adjusted for inflation so it can be counted at its current value

1 FICA FEEDER
You feed the Social Security machine every year you work

WHAT YOU CAN EXPECT

Although the dollar amount of your benefit reflects your average earnings, the percentage of earnings your benefit will replace goes down as your earned income goes up. That's in keeping with Social Security's mission of providing a basic level of financial support.

You can use the chart to the right to find an **estimate** of the dollar benefit you would get, based on your age and salary. If you retire at 65 in 2004 and had steady earnings of $30,000 a year, you'll receive a benefit of $1,056, or about 42% of your salary. You can project the percentage of your income that will be replaced using the following formula:

$$\frac{\text{Monthly benefit} \times 12}{\text{Annual wage}} = \text{\% annual income}$$

for example

$$\frac{\$1,056 \times 12}{\$30,000} = \frac{\$12,672}{\$30,000} = 42.2\%$$

Or, you can compute your own benefit estimate if you visit the Social Security home page, www.ssa.gov.

Of course, the younger you are, the less accurate the benefit projections may be because it's difficult to predict what will happen to the economy.

EXAMPLES OF BENEFITS ESTIMATES AT FULL RETIREMENT

Average Earnings	Current Age		
	42	52	62
20K	843	828	812
30K	1,102	1,080	1,056
40K	1,361	1,332	1,300
50K	1,507	1,490	1,464
60K+	1,628	1,608	1,555

THE INFLATION ISSUE

Unlike most pensions, Social Security benefits are adjusted for inflation. As well as increasing the amount of earnings subject to tax and the amount you have to earn to qualify for credits, the SSA also recalculates the amount you get every year, using a percentage of your basic benefit amount. The new amount is never less than the year before, though the rate of increase varies to reflect changes in the cost of living.

These cost of living adjustments, or **COLAs**, begin when you're 62. If you wait until you reach full retirement age to start collecting, those COLAs are added to the base amount on which your benefit is figured. The larger benefit payments you will receive can be an incentive to wait to apply for your benefits.

3 BENEFIT BALANCER
Your basic benefit rate is permanent, though what you get may be more or less, depending on when you collect

4 COLA COLLECTOR
Every year your benefit is increased to adjust for increases in the cost of living

5 BENEFIT BIN
Your benefit is based on your basic rate, adjusted for inflation and the age at which you begin to collect

When to Apply

When you're ready to collect, you have to ask for your money.

Your Social Security benefit won't automatically appear in your mailbox the day you're eligible. You'll have to ask the SSA to start paying, and you'll have to provide evidence that you qualify. The same material you used to open your account can be used here, too: birth or baptismal certificates, passports, naturalization papers, or other official documents. You may also need a copy of your most recent W-2 form or tax return. Your local Social Security office can answer the questions you have, or you can call 800-772-1213. The SSA advises you not to delay your application because you don't have the right documentation, or aren't sure what you need. Once you start the process, they'll help you get hold of the information.

Changes in Social Security Retirement-Age Provisions

Year of Birth	Attainment of Age 62	Starting Age for Full Benefits (Year/Months)	Credit for Each Year of Delayed Retirement	Age-62 Benefit as % of PIA
1938	2000	65/2	6.5%	79.2%
1939	2001	65/4	7.0%	78.3%
1940	2002	65/6	7.0%	77.5%
1941	2003	65/8	7.5%	76.7%
1942	2004	65/10	7.5%	75.8%
1943-54	2005-16	66/0	8.0%	75.0%
1955	2017	66/2	8.0%	74.2%
1956	2018	66/4	8.0%	73.3%
1957	2019	66/6	8.0%	72.5%
1958	2020	66/8	8.0%	71.7%
1959	2021	66/10	8.0%	70.8%
1960+	2022+	67/0	8.0%	70.0%

SPREADING THE WEALTH

You can start collecting Social Security as early as 62 or as late as 70. The earlier you begin, the smaller the annual amount you get. And the later you start, the larger your payments. The underlying principle the SSA has adopted in providing these options is trying to equalize the lifetime value of the benefits.

If you must be older than 65 to receive full benefits, you can still start collecting at 62, but the percentage of full payment gradually drops from 80% to 70%. Just the opposite is true if you wait until 70.

Your benefit is larger, but chances are you will collect for fewer years.

The general feeling is that you should be collecting as soon as you're eligible. It will take between 12 and 17 years—until you're nearly 80—for the larger amount you would have gotten at full retirement age to add up to more money.

Of course, if you have the option of continuing to work, the added income during those extra years will probably be more than the Social Security payments you would have received. And if your salary increases, the base amount of your benefit will increase as well.

A LONGER ROW TO HOE

The age for getting full benefits is gradually increasing. If you were born before 1938, you still qualify for full benefits at age 65. But anyone born in 1938 has to be 65 and two months, anyone born in 1939 has to be 65 and four months, and so on. As this chart shows, full retirement age inches up to 66 for people born between 1943 and 1954 and to 67 for anyone born after 1960.

PATIENCE HAS ITS REWARDS

People who wait to begin collecting because they are still working get a bonus. If they were born before 1938, they get between 3% and 4% a year added on to their basic benefit for each year they wait between age 65 and age 70. But people born in 1943 or after, who have to be age 66 to get full benefits, will get an extra 8% a year more than their primary insurance amount (PIA), or full benefit. There's no point, though, in waiting past 70, because the amount you're eligible for won't increase any more.

RECEIVING THE MONEY

Once you're ready to collect, you can choose how you want to get the money. The SSA will mail you a check—which should arrive on the third of every month—or they'll deposit it directly in your checking or savings account. Most people—more than 77%—opt for direct deposit. It's safer, quicker, and usually more convenient than getting a check. It's also cheaper for the government.

To use the direct deposit option, all you need is something that shows your bank and

APPLYING FOR BENEFITS

The SSA suggests that you discuss applying for Social Security benefits in the year before you actually plan to retire. Since there are several options for timing retirement and the start of your benefits, the SSA can help you figure out the choice that will work best for you. You have three basic choices:

- **Retiring early, any time after age 62**
- **Retiring at full retirement age, which has historically been 65**
- **Postponing retirement past 65**

FOR INFORMATION CALL
1-800-772-1213

THE OTHER ISSUES

Chances are there are several factors behind choosing the age at which you apply for retirement benefits. Your health, your plans for the future, or an incentive your employer offers for leaving your job early can make a difference. So can the type of job you have and whether or not you plan to go on working.

On the other hand, once you start collecting Social Security there are limits on the amount you can earn between ages 62 and 65 before you start losing some of your benefit. For many people, who need or want to go on working, postponing taking the benefits makes sense. But, once you retire, you should apply right away. If you don't need the money for living expenses, you can invest it.

77.2%
DIRECT DEPOSIT

22.8%
IN THE MAIL

account number, like a checkbook, a passbook or a bank statement.

People who have moved into retirement or nursing homes, or who aren't managing their own finances, can have their money deposited in a custodial account. That way, the benefit can be used directly for their care.

Working after Retirement

There's no law against working after you retire—but there are limits on what you can earn.

To insure Social Security's integrity as a source of basic financial support after retirement, there are limits on what you can earn while collecting your payments before you turn 65. After 65, you can earn as much as you want and still get the full amount you're entitled to.

You can also collect your full benefit if you receive special payments after you retire that you actually earned beforehand. Typical examples include accumulated vacation pay, sales commissions, and deferred salary. The same rule applies to some self-employment income. According to Social Security, some people entitled to receive benefits postpone them unnecessarily because of payments like these.

LETTING SOCIAL SECURITY KNOW

If you're working, you're required to let the Social Security Administration know. You have to estimate your earnings using a special form called **Annual Report of Earnings**. The Social Security Administration reduces the number of monthly checks you get in the following year, based on that earnings estimate.

If you earn less than you estimated, you'll get a check to cover what you're owed. But if you earn more, you have to pay back the difference between what you got and what you were entitled to, either in a lump sum or installments. When your taxes are due in April, you submit form SSA-777 and a copy of your tax return to the Social Security Administration to verify your earnings.

The worst-case situation is failing to report that you're working and then going over the limit. You'll have to pay a penalty as well as send back any over-payment you got.

THE LIMITS

If you're receiving Social Security, there may be a fixed amount you can earn each year without losing some of your benefit. As a rule, the cap goes up each year to reflect increases in the cost of living, and is keyed to the average earnings of all employees in the country.

The amount also changes depending on how old you are. In 2004, you could earn $11,640 if you were between 62 and 64, and up to $31,080 if you reached full retirement age during the year, and still get full benefits.

THE CONSEQUENCES

The consequences of earning more than the limit is fewer checks from Social Security. Before you turn 65, you lose $1 for every $2 over the limit, and the year you reached full retirement age you lose $1 for every $3 over the limit.

However, the limits apply only to earned income, not pensions, annuities, investment earnings, or any government benefits.

If you were 62–64, and receiving about $800 a month, you'd get your first check in June. At the end of the year, based on your actual earnings, SSA might owe you money, or you might owe the SSA.

DOES IT PAY TO WORK?

It's a judgment call, if the amount you earn is going to reduce your benefit significantly. In general, though, if your earnings are low enough to allow you to get any benefit while you're working, you make out better taking what you're entitled to. For example, suppose you're 63, get a monthly benefit of $1,050 a month ($12,600 a year) and earn $19,100 a year. You'd still get over 70% of your benefit. Here's how:

Social Security says if you work over 45 hours a month, you're <u>not</u> retired.

Social Security says if you work less than 15 hours a month, you're <u>retired</u>.

YOUR AGE	MAXIMUM EARNINGS FOR FULL BENEFITS
62–64	$11,640
65	$31,080
65 and over	NO LIMIT

IF YOUR INCOME IS $19,100

	UNDER 65
Amount over limit	$ 7,460
Reduced by ½	÷ 2
Benefit reduced by	$ 3,730

$ 19,100	Earnings
− 11,640	Earnings limit
$ 7,460	Excess earning
÷ 2	Reduced by ½
$ 3,730	Benefit reduction
÷ 12,600	Original benefit
29.6%	Reduction

CHANGING YOUR MIND

It is true that once you begin receiving your Social Security payments you're locked into the base amount. But you can change your mind about getting the payments, pay back the total amount you've received and start over again— at a higher base—later on.

For example, if you retire and begin to receive benefits when you're 62 but are offered a position that's too good to turn down, you can stop your Social Security payments. As long as you repay any benefits you got, you can start again with a clean slate when you're ready to quit working for good. Whatever you've earned in the period when you returned to work can increase the amount you're eligible to receive.

SPECIAL RULES

If you retire in the middle of the year, you might have already exceeded the annual earnings limit. So in the year you retire, special rules apply. You can get the full benefit you're entitled to in any month that you're actually retired, no matter what you earned earlier in the year.

But once the Social Security payments start, you can't earn more than $\frac{1}{12}$ of the maximum earnings limit for your age. If you go over that limit in any month, you lose the entire benefit for that month. But the next month you start over.

WHAT RETIRED MEANS

When your income is from self-employment, defining retirement is a little tricky. The SSA uses the number of hours you spend working during a month as the measuring stick. If you work fewer than 15 hours, you're considered retired. If you work more than 45 hours, you're definitely not. And then there's the gray area in between, when the quality of the work you do, as well as the time you spend doing it, has to be considered.

The rules are complex. The SSA invites people in that situation to get in touch with a representative for specific information about the way their benefits are calculated.

Family Coverage

Social Security benefits are a family affair, as long as one person qualifies for coverage.

When you qualify for Social Security retirement benefits, you get them for as long as you live. What's more, your spouse and certain dependents, including your young or disabled children can collect as well, both while you're collecting and after your death.

WHOSE BENEFIT ANYWAY?

If you and your spouse each qualify for benefits, you each collect on your own account when you retire. Not only does it give you more flexibility about when to retire, but it might add up to a larger benefit, especially if your earnings were about the same.

But if the total you get individually adds up to less than you would receive if one of you collected as a dependent spouse, Social Security makes up the difference, as this example shows.

for example		
	Individual benefits only	Spousal benefits from one account
You	$1,128	$1,128
Your spouse	415	564
Total benefit	$1,543	$1,692

Social Security would make up the $149 difference, so your benefit would be $1,692.

SWITCHING GEARS

The choice between getting your own benefit or your spousal survivor benefits is one of those rare situations in retirement planning where you can change your mind. Your initial decision doesn't lock you in, even after you've begun receiving benefits.

If you'd get a larger payment by switching—usually from what you get on your own to what you'd get as your spouse's survivor—all you have to do is request the change and be able to prove your marital status and age.

When you switch, your new benefit is reduced by the amount you've already received in your own name. The SSA will tell you what the new amount is, so you can decide whether switching pays.

THE GENERAL RULES

Who Is Eligible

SPOUSE
- Your spouse must be at least 62 to collect, unless he or she is caring for your child who's younger than 16, or disabled and receiving Social Security benefits

CHILDREN

DISABLED CHILDREN

BENEFIT LIMITS

There is a limit to what Social Security will pay to your family—usually between 150% and 180% of your benefit. Here's how the limit works:

Suppose your benefit is $1,000 a month and you and your spouse have three children under 16 when you retire. With no limits, your family would get a total of $3,000 (your $1,000 plus $500 for each of the others). With the limits in place, the most your family would get would be $1,800. But it's never your benefit that's cut. The difference comes out of what your dependents receive.

180% Family benefits — Upper limit for family benefits—180% of base benefit

100% Base benefit

FORMER FAMILIES

If you're divorced, you may be eligible for Social Security retirement benefits based on your former spouse's earnings. You're entitled to the same benefits you would have received—50% at full retirement age—if you'd stayed married. You may also be able to start collecting at 62 even if your ex-spouse is still working, provided you have been divorced for at least two years, and the worker is 62.

The SSA imposes these conditions to collect on a divorced spouse's earnings:

You were married for at least ten years, you aren't remarried, and you're not eligible for an equal or larger benefit based on your own or someone else's earnings.

YOU'RE ALL COVERED

If your ex-spouse is getting Social Security benefits based on your record, it doesn't reduce the amount you and your current family, if you've remarried, are entitled to. And there are no limits to the number of former spouses entitled to a benefit based on your contributions, as long as you've been married to each of them the required length of time.

When you apply for benefits for your dependents, you'll have to prove your relationship and how old they are. You'll also have to keep this rule in mind: Your spouse and other dependents aren't eligible for benefits until you start collecting yours. For example, a 66-year-old husband can't collect spousal benefits if his wife is still working.

When They Are Eligible

- Spouses who begin collecting at 65, or those who are taking care of minor or disabled children are entitled to 50% of your benefit amount
- If your spouse starts to collect between 62 and 65, though, and there are no eligible children, the benefit is reduced a small percentage each month, currently to a floor of 37.5% at 62
- A spouse who isn't 62 when your last child turns 16 loses eligibility until turning 62

- Children are eligible for family benefits when you retire if they're under 18 (or under 19 if they're still in high school full-time); as your children reach 18, they lose their eligibility

- Children are eligible if they're disabled, as long as the disability occurred before they were 22

How Much the Benefit Will Be

- Spouses are eligible for 50% of your full retirement benefit at age 65, reduced slightly for each month before that, currently to a floor of 37.5% at 62

- Children are eligible for 50% of your full retirement benefit

Survivor Benefits

The Social Security you leave behind is a legacy your survivors can be sure they'll receive.

While Social Security is designed to provide basic financial security after you retire, an equally important role is providing an income for your survivors no matter what age you are when you die. Your widow or widower, your young or disabled children, parents who were dependent on you, and, in certain circumstances, your divorced former spouse are entitled to survivor benefits.

QUALIFYING FOR BENEFITS

To provide benefits for your survivors, you must accumulate enough credits while you're working. You qualify either by having the full number required for your age, or by being currently insured, having earned at least six credits in the three years before your death. That means if you work for at least one and a half of the three years before your death, your minor children—and your spouse who cares for them—will still be covered.

Your age determines the number of credits you need to be fully qualified. It's one for every year between the year you turn 21 and the year before you die or turn 61, whichever comes first. For example, if you were born in 1948, and died in 2001, you would have needed 31 credits. When you turn 61, in 2009, you'll need 40 credits.

THE CREDITS YOU NEED

The year before your death
− The year you turn 21

= Credits needed for survivor benefits

for example

	2000	The year before your death
−	1969	The year you turn 21
=	31	Credits needed for survivor benefits

APPLYING FOR BENEFITS

If you're a survivor who's eligible for Social Security benefits, you should apply immediately. You'll need a copy of the insured person's death certificate, and evidence of your age, relationship, and marital situation.

Your deceased spouse or parent is not entitled to a Social Security benefit for the month he or she dies. When the payment is made, on the third of the next month, you should return it to the SSA.

DEATH BENEFIT

If you have the credits you need to provide benefits for your survivors, Social Security also makes a one-time payment to your spouse or minor children at the time of your death. Although there are no rules about what the money must be used for, it's often described as a funeral benefit.

WHAT ABOUT REMARRIAGE?

If you're getting survivor benefits, you won't lose them if you remarry after you're 60, or 50 if you're disabled. But if you're eligible for a larger benefit based on your new spouse's earnings record, that takes

THE GENERAL RULES

Who is Eligible

WIDOWS AND WIDOWERS
- At age 60, or 50 if disabled
- Married at least 9 months
- Not remarried before age 60, or 50 if disabled
- Taking care of children under 16, or disabled children who are receiving Social Security benefits

CHILDREN
- Unmarried
- Under 18 (or 19 if full-time high school students)
- Disabled before age 22

PARENTS
- Dependent on covered worker for more than half their support
- Age 62 or more

FORMER SPOUSES
- At age 60, 50 if disabled
- Married to covered worker for at least 10 years
- Unmarried at time of application
- Taking care of children under 16, or disabled children receiving Social Security benefits (no length of marriage rule)

precedence. It isn't a question of loyalty or affection so much as one of economics. With Social Security, the smart decision is the one that pays the most.

If you remarry when your children are younger than 18, they will continue to receive benefits until they are too old to be eligible. Their status as survivors is not affected by your marriage.

BENEFITS AFTER RETIREMENT

If your spouse is receiving retirement benefits when he or she dies, you're entitled as a survivor to 100% of your spouse's Social Security payment. For example, if

NON-TRADITIONAL FAMILIES

So far, Social Security has not extended coverage to non-traditional family relationships. You must be legally married or a blood relative to qualify as a survivor. But the history of Social Security demonstrates that it has changed with the times, providing benefits for divorced people, for example, when divorce became a fact of life. So a change in the definition of family membership is possible, if not immediately likely.

the basic benefit was $1,200 and you were getting an additional $600, you're eligible for $1,200 as a surviving spouse.

At your spouse's death, you can switch from collecting on your own account to collecting as a survivor if it means you're eligible for a larger benefit. The SSA will calculate the amount for you.

The chart below gives you an overview of who's eligible for survivor benefits and how much they're entitled to. Since there are many exceptions to the general rules, your situation may be different. The SSA can explain where you stand.

What the Benefits Are	Other Provisions
• 100% of covered worker's basic benefit for coverage beginning at 65, about 83% at 62 and about 72% at 60 • About 72% for disabled spouses who begin collecting between 50 and 59 • 75% of basic benefit while caring for minor or disabled children	• Surviving spouses earning more than the limit Social Security allows are eligible for benefits, though deductions are imposed; Children under 18 still eligible • Surviving spouses who remarry after 60 (or 50 if disabled) may still collect
• 75% of parent's basic benefit	• Children over 18 (or 19 in certain cases) are no longer eligible even if full-time college students • Disabled children continue to be eligible
• 82.5% for one parent; 75% each for two parents	
• 100% of covered worker's basic benefit for coverage beginning at 65, about 83% at 62, and about 72% at 60 • About 72% for disabled spouses who begin collecting between 50 and 59 • 75% of basic benefit while caring for minor or disabled children	• Former spouses earning more than the limit Social Security allows are not eligible for benefits, though children under 18 continue to be eligible • Former spouses who remarry after 60 (or 50 if disabled) may still collect

There's a monthly limit on the total amount a family receives, though, just as there is with retirement benefits.

Disability Benefits

Disability insurance is the most complicated Social Security program.

Controversy swirls around the disability insurance program. Some people argue that it's too expensive because it's too generous. Others insist that people who ought to be receiving benefits are left out in the cold.

For example, rules governing benefits paid to disabled children and to people who are disabled because of drug addiction or alcoholism are more restrictive than they once were. In the latter, for example, rehabilitation treatment is required and there's a time limit for receiving benefits.

SOCIAL SECURITY ADMINISTRATION
DISABILITY DETERMINATION SERVICE

Applicant Checklist

- [ ] All medical records
- [ ] Insurance history
- [ ] Tax returns
- [ ] Employment records, past 15 years
- [ ] Proof of age

DEFINING A DISABILITY

The SSA calls its definition of disability "strict." No benefits are paid unless you're unable to work at your former job or adapt to a new one that pays more than the monthly minimum that's reset each year. Just because you're considered disabled by your employer or your doctor doesn't mean you're eligible for Social Security benefits. The decision rests with the **Disability Determination Service** in the state where you live.

SOCIAL SECURITY PAYS OUT ABOUT $67.2 BILLION IN DISABILITY BENEFITS TO 7.8 MILLION PEOPLE

Applications for benefits continue to increase each year, putting a strain on the program's financial resources.

Despite the restrictions and the red tape, disability applications and awards are increasing. The average age of disability recipients is declining. Each year, almost 1.5 million disabled workers and their dependents qualify for new awards.

APPLYING FOR BENEFITS

The more quickly you apply for disability benefits, the better. It takes longer to process a disability claim—about four months—than a claim for retirement or survivor benefits. Plus you have to supply detailed medical and work records. The SSA wants to know, for example, where you worked for the 15 years before you were disabled.

If your claim is approved—and only about a third are the first time around—payments can begin in the sixth full month after you were disabled. For example, if you have a stroke in June, you would be eligible for benefits in December and the payment would arrive on January 3. Disability claims for children, or for people eligible for SSI benefits, have no waiting period.

WAIT
TILL YOUR NAME IS CALLED

BEING ELIGIBLE

You are eligible for disability benefits if you have earned enough credits while you're working. You need an increasing number of credits, based on your age, to a maximum of 40 at age 62, just as you do for survivor benefits. But to qualify for disability coverage, you must earn 20 of those credits in the ten years immediately before you are disabled.

If you're disabled but don't have enough Social Security credits, you might qualify for Supplemental Security Income (SSI) if you have a small income and few assets.

FIGURING YOUR BENEFIT

The SSA estimates the disability benefit you'd be eligible for when it provides your annual Social Security Statement. The amount is based on:

- **Your age at the time you're disabled**
- **Your earnings record**

Once you've begun to receive payments, your basic benefit doesn't change no matter how many years you're eligible to collect. You do get cost of living adjustments though. Social Security doesn't recognize a partial disability, or make partial payments. If you qualify, you get the amount you're entitled to until you recover or improve enough to go back to work.

If you're eligible for other benefits, like Workers' Compensation, you may get less from Social Security (or the other way around). That's because all your disability payments together can't add up to more than 80% of your average recent earnings. But after 24 months of disability benefits, you are eligible for Medicare.

THE APPEALS PROCESS

If the SSA rules you're not eligible for disability benefits, you can appeal the decision. Historically, the administrative law judges working for the SSA have reversed more than half of the rejected applications. If the ruling goes against you internally, and you believe you have a case, you can take it to an Appeals Council and finally to Federal District Court.

You May Be Disabled if You Have:

- **Sight loss**
- **Chronic arthritis**
- **Loss of limbs**
- **AIDS or HIV infection**
- **Multiple personality**
- **Schizophrenia**
- **Kidney failure**
- **Mental retardation**
- **Heart disease**
- **Emphysema**
- **Stroke**
- **Cancer**
- **Chronic obesity**
- **Paralysis**

or other conditions

But Only if the SSA Says You Are.

A LONG HISTORY

The original disability pensions in the U.S. date back to 1636, when the Massachusetts Bay Colony began supporting its injured soldiers. More than 300 years later, in 1957, Social Security instituted a disability program for workers over 50 and extended it three years later to include everyone who qualified. In 2004, disability payments accounted for about 19% of all Social Security benefits.

Taxing Benefits

The tax on benefits makes economic sense, but it's not very popular with the 20% who pay it.

The law on taxing benefits is fairly simple: If your total income for the year hits a certain level, you owe income taxes on 50% of your Social Security benefit. And if your income hits an even higher level, you owe taxes on 85% of your benefit.

WHAT IS THIS BENEFIT ANYWAY

The underlying question is, should everybody who pays Social Security taxes get retirement benefits? Or should the benefits go only to people who need them to live on?

Because everyone who works must contribute to the system, the idea of using a means test to decide who gets benefits has been rejected—at least so far.

Using a means test, only people whose income falls below a certain level would qualify for benefits. If you're in good financial shape, the argument goes, why do you need the benefits? But if you're not going to get anything back, why should you put anything in? And doesn't using money that everyone must contribute to support only some of the people change the nature

of the whole Social Security program? The current solution has been to tax some of the benefits of some of the people, but it hasn't answered the pressing questions.

The 50 (or 85) Percent Solution

ALL IN THE NUMBERS

You can figure out whether you'll have to pay income taxes on part of your Social Security benefit by using this workchart.

Compare the total on line 6 with the income limits for your filing status in the chart to the right. If the total is less, you don't owe taxes on any of your Social Security benefits.

		for example:
1	Income from Box 5 of SSA 1099 (if you got more than one SSA-1099 include the combined total)	$ 21,600
2	Divide by amount in line 1 by 2	÷ 2
3	Half of Social Security	= $ 10,800
4	Income from pensions, wages, dividends, taxable interest and other sources	+ $ 24,000
5	Income from tax-exempt interest and other non-taxable income	+ $ 4,000
6	Add lines 3–5	= $ 38,800

STARTING A TREND OR TWO

When women made up a smaller segment of the work force, they briefly enjoyed a special privilege: collecting their Society Security benefit earlier. From 1956 to 1961, women, but not men, had the option of retiring with benefits at age 62. By 1961, men were given the same option, and the trend toward earlier retirement was on a roll. Only 2% of those eligible took advantage of the offer in 1956, but since 1994 it's been nearly 70%.

Men, on average, still qualify for larger individual retirement awards, but the proportion of women among retired-worker beneficiaries has quadrupled since 1940, and the proportion of women qualifying only as dependents has declined significantly.

COUNTING YOUR INCOME

In figuring whether you owe tax on your benefits, you add everything you receive—including tax-exempt interest on municipal bonds and certain other income that you don't normally have to include in your taxable income. What's still excluded is return of investment principal in annuity payments.

- Salary
- Pensions
- Taxable investment income
- Tax-exempt income from municipal bonds
- Overseas earnings
- Gambling, lottery winnings
- Tips
- Royalties, rents
- IRA withdrawals

If the total is higher, you include a percentage of your benefit—either 50% or 85%—as part of your taxable income on your tax return. In cases where your income is only slightly greater than the limit, you pay tax on less than the full 50% or 85%. The IRS provides a worksheet you can use to figure out exactly how much you must add to your taxable income.

If you pay estimated taxes, you'll have to include enough to cover what you'll owe on your Social Security benefits.

FILING STATUS	INCOME LEVEL	
SINGLE	$25,000	$34,000
MARRIED, LIVING APART WITH SEPARATE RETURNS	$25,000	$34,000
MARRIED, FILING JOINTLY	$32,000	$44,000
MARRIED, WITH SEPARATE RETURNS	ANY INCOME	ANY INCOME

50% OF YOUR BENEFIT WILL BE TAXED

85% OF YOUR BENEFIT WILL BE TAXED

OTHER OPTIONS

If your income falls close to or within the limits that would subject part of the benefit to taxation, you may be able to plan ahead so that some years you're subjected to tax and other years you're not. For example, by timing the date that U.S. Treasury bills mature, or postponing selling some stock, you might be able to bunch income in one year—and pay the tax—while keeping it under the limits in another.

A WORKING SPOUSE

When you apply for retirement benefits based on your work record, your right to collect is unrelated to whether or not your spouse is working. When you reach retirement age you can collect. But when it comes to figuring whether or not part of your Social Security benefit will be taxed, your spouse's income makes a big difference.

For example, if a man retires at 65 and is entitled to a benefit of $1,128 a month, that's what he gets even if his wife is earning $65,000. But at tax time, their joint income will be way over the level that requires them to pay tax on 85% of his Social Security benefit.

Unless they're married but permanently living apart, there's no way to avoid the tax by filing separate returns. As the chart shows, married couples filing separately pay tax on half their Social Security benefit no matter what their income—just to eliminate this tax-saving option.

When your spouse is eligible for benefits and earning only enough to push the joint income over the limit, it might pay to calculate tax liability both ways, to figure out if it makes more sense financially for both of you to retire because your taxes will be significantly less.

Personal Investing Goals

Chances are, living the life you want after you retire will depend on your investment income.

In many ways, investing for retirement is just like investing for any other reason. You invest your **principal,** or the money you have, to earn more money, which you can use to pay your bills, buy something you want, or make a new investment. But when you're investing for long-term financial security, there's no fixed moment when you need the money. Instead, it's a continuous process.

That means you always have to think about doing three things:

- **Making your investment grow**
- **Producing income**
- **Preserving your principal**

FIRST THINGS FIRST

If you're putting money into a tax-deferred savings plan, you're already investing for retirement in one of the most potentially productive ways you can. That contribution may be most, or even all, of what you feel you can put away. Yet, the truth is, being able to afford the kind of retirement you want will depend—in most cases—on the personal investments you make in addition to the money you put in tax-deferred plans. If you don't start until retirement is within sight, it's tough to invest enough to produce the income you'll need.

THE GROWTH STAGE

Growth is the first order of business, and investments may grow in many ways.

- You can beef up your principal on a regular basis by contributing a percentage of your income to your investment pool or contributing the maximum to an IRA

- You can reinvest your investment earnings rather than spend them, either by using an official plan offered by a mutual fund or stock reinvestment program, or by putting all your interest and dividend payments into a special investment account

- You can invest your money in **equity** products like stocks and stock mutual funds, though growth isn't guaranteed, and they could also lose value

- You can **diversify,** or put your money into a variety of investments, to take advantage of ups and downs in the stock market and interest rates

WHAT YOU CAN'T KNOW CAN HURT YOU

You can't actually know how much you'll need when you retire, or what the state of the economy will be then. You can get a sense if you can project your salary increases, the rate of inflation, and how much you'll be paying in taxes 10, 20, or 30 years in the future.

There's a certain element of guesswork in any projection, even a computer-generated one. The only thing you can tell for certain is that if you don't invest, you won't have what you need.

COMING UP SHORT

Most experts agree that you need 80% of your preretirement income after you retire if you want to maintain a similar style of living. Social Security benefits and, in some cases, an employer sponsored pension, will supply some of what you need.

For example, if you're earning $75,000 when you retire, your financial picture might look like this.

$	75,000	Pre-retirement income
x	.80	
= $	60,000	Post retirement need
–	15,600	Social Security benefits
–	22,500	Pension benefits
= $	21,900	**FIRST YEAR INCOME SHORTFALL**

MAKING UP THE DIFFERENCE

You might go on working part-time — though that may not be your idea of retirement. The other option — short of winning the lottery — is a regular income from the investments you've built up over the years. The more carefully you've diversified those investments, the more likely it is that you can count on them to produce the earnings you'll need. Here are three examples of ways you might do it.

1

$	8,250	$150,000 Treasury bonds paying 5.5%
+	7,500	$150,000 IRA withdrawal at 5%
+	6,930	Liquidating 4.5% of a $154,000 stock portfolio
= $	22,680	**INCOME FROM INVESTING**

2

$	10,000	$200,000 SEP-IRA withdrawn at 5%
+	1,500	$75,000 in stock yielding 2%
+	11,500	Maturing certificate of deposit (CD)
= $	23,000	**INCOME FROM INVESTING**

3

$	4,200	Rental on real estate holdings
+	4,500	Liquidating 5% of a $90,000 stock portfolio
+	13,750	$275,000 Keogh plan withdrawn at 5%
= $	22,450	**INCOME FROM INVESTING**

THE INCOME STAGE

Income-producing investments are especially important when you need the money to live on, typically after you retire. For example, the interest on a bond or the dividends from a stock help cover day-to-day expenses. Since those payments are made regularly, usually quarterly or semi-annually, you can plan on them. You can also time certain investments, like certificates of deposit or certain bonds, to mature on a specific schedule, to replenish your cash reserve or meet anticipated expenses.

Income from your investments also produces a regular source of new investment money. Or, you can plan to spend a certain amount and reinvest the rest.

THE PRESERVATION STAGE

If you're living on the income your investments provide, you've got a vested interest in making sure they don't shrink in value or, worse yet, disappear altogether. Curiously, the

best preservation technique is often to concentrate on growth—slower, safer growth than you were looking for when you first began to build your nest egg, but growth nonetheless. Money buried in the backyard, or earning minimal interest in a savings account, doesn't keep its value. In fact, because of inflation, it shrinks. That's one of the biggest threats to your financial security.

The Impact of Inflation

A dollar buys less as inflation eats away at its value.

Inflation is an erosion of money's value. The amount of erosion varies—in some years the rate of inflation is higher than in others. But the effect of inflation never changes: The cost of living keeps going up, so you need more money just to stay even.

INFLATION PROTECTION

You can't stop inflation, but you can protect yourself against it by investing for growth. Generally speaking, that means putting at least some of your money into stocks and stock mutual funds. Since 1926, **equity** investments have returned an average of over 10% a year, while the inflation rate in the same period averaged around 3%.

The rule of thumb is that you need to earn more than the current inflation rate on your combined investments to get ahead. That's because your **real rate of growth** is what remains after subtracting the inflation rate from your rate of return. For example, if inflation is running at 3%, your goal is 4% or better: A 4% return minus 3% inflation equals a 1% real return before taxes. CDs, money market accounts, and other cash investments rarely pay significantly more than inflation and often pay less. That's why you need to invest your money in other ways.

The higher the real rate of return you're earning on your combined investments, the better your defense against the effects of inflation.

The standard pension fund mix of 60% invested in stocks, 30% in bonds, and 10% in cash has regularly earned at least four percentage points over the inflation rate, which is one of the reasons that companies have been able to meet their pension obligations. As a rule, if the bulk of your investments isn't diversified, you'll probably find yourself earning less than the inflation rate over the long term.

INFLATION HAPPENS

Though unexpected changes in world politics, like a war or an oil embargo, can cause a sudden leap in prices, inflation isn't random or arbitrary.

Historically, it has been linked to a country's economy. In periods of strong growth, inflation increased, and when things cooled off, inflation slowed. Of course, there are exceptions to the rule. Inflation has sometimes remained stable as an economy expanded, as it did in the 1990s. But experts can't always explain why, or predict whether such exceptions will recur in the future.

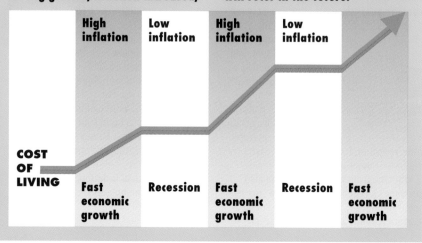

	High inflation	Low inflation	High inflation	Low inflation	
COST OF LIVING	Fast economic growth	Recession	Fast economic growth	Recession	Fast economic growth

A NON-SCIENTIFIC LOOK AT THE EVER-DIMINISHING BUYING POWER OF THE DOLLAR

1963   2004*

CUP OF COFFEE
$.10 $.75

LUXURY CAR
$2,800 $48,000

PAIR OF SNEAKERS
$4.95 $89.95

STAMP
$.05 $.37

NEWSPAPER
$.10 $1.00

NYC SUBWAY FARE
$.15 $2.00

GALLON OF MILK
$1.80 $3.02

GALLON OF GAS
$.30 $1.95

MOVIE TICKET
$.86 $6.03

*Statistics available as of 8/31/04

THE RULE OF 72

To figure out how fast your money is losing its value, you can use the rule of 72. Just divide 72 by the current inflation rate to find the number of years it will take prices to double. For example, if the rate is 3%, prices will double in 24 years: The movie ticket that costs $8.50 in 2004 will cost $17 in 2028. (One bright spot, though: If you've retired by 2028, you'll probably be eligible for a senior citizen discount.)

To figure the impact of higher inflation rates on your cost of living, you can use the same rule. If inflation were running at 10%, that movie ticket would double in just over seven years.

Inflation also erodes what money is worth. If the rate stays a relatively modest 3%, the $100 you have today will buy less

$$\frac{72}{\text{Current inflation rate}} = \text{Number of years until prices are doubled}$$

for example

$$\frac{72}{3} = \text{24 years until a pair of sneakers will cost}$$

$179.90

than half the amount in 12 years that it buys now, and next to nothing in 24. Since many people live at least 24 years after they retire, you can see why inflation is a matter for concern.

WHAT GOES UP

Inflation creates serious problems for people living on fixed incomes, such as pensions, annuity payments, or interest on bonds. A fixed income means that the dollar amount of the payment is set from the beginning and does not change. A $10,000 bond paying 5.5% will give you $550 a year for as long as you hold it. That means your buying power will decline.

The flip side of inflation's negative effect is that bonds, CDs, and bank accounts pay higher interest during periods of high inflation, providing a healthy current return even though the real return may still be too low to produce growth.

Many retired people see their interest income decline dramatically during extended periods of minimal inflation and low interest rates. When bonds that pay high rates—perhaps 8% or more—mature, new ones may pay only 5% or so, a huge decline for people depending on interest earnings to pay their bills.

A Winning Strategy

You've got a better chance at the winning shot in the investment game if you've figured out a strategy.

Random buying—a few stocks here, a bond there—rarely produces enough return to provide the extra income you'll need for retirement. Jumping into what's hot works the same way, since usually by the time you hear an investment is hot, it's started to cool off.

THE HEART OF THE MATTER

It's not that there's a single right way for making money with your investments. There are several ways that often work well, and that you can adapt to suit your needs and your resources. To be a successful investor, you need a sense of what you want to accomplish—a goal—and a plan, or strategy, for getting there.

THE MONEY YOU HAVE TO INVEST

IMPATIENT— OUT OF MARKET TOO SOON

RANDOM BUYING

Whatever strategy you adopt in investing for retirement, the same three rules apply:

START EARLY

STICK WITH IT

SALT AWAY AS MUCH AS YOU CAN

BORROWING FOR NOW

If you need cash before you retire, it may make more sense to borrow against your investments than to sell them or withdraw part of the money. It doesn't work with everything—you can't borrow against a mutual fund, for instance. But you can borrow against brokerage accounts, some pension or retirement plans, and insurance policies.

By borrowing, you avoid the capital gains or income taxes that might be due and any penalties you would have to pay for early withdrawal. While you do have to pay the amount back, borrowing can solve a short-term problem without diverting your long-term strategy.

DRAWING ON PRINCIPAL

While preserving principal is critical while you're investing for retirement, there's nothing wrong with using some of the principal—say 5% a year—*after* you retire. But, you need a plan for tapping your resources, similar to a withdrawal schedule for your IRA or Keogh, and a sense of which investments to liquidate.

A maturing CD, for example, can become a source of current income. When it comes due, you can deposit the principal in a money market mutual fund or savings account to draw on as you need cash. That might be smarter than withdrawing money from an investment that's doing well, like a stock fund, or selling real estate when prices are low.

A PLAN, NOT A STRAITJACKET

As an investor, you need to be flexible. Economic trends change, so you have to modify your plan from time to time. You'll come up short, for example, if you keep lots of money in certificates of deposit (CDs) if the interest they offer is only as good as the return on a money market account. Just because CDs are a smart investment at one time doesn't mean they always are. Or, for that matter, does it mean that they won't be a wise choice again.

When you're investing for retirement, it usually makes sense to shift your strategy as you get closer to actually leaving the workforce—from concentrating primarily on growth to thinking about producing income. In your 30s and 40s, you can take more chances with your investments, since you'll still have time to make up for mistakes or market losses. But a big loss in your 60s can be hard to recover from.

THE MONEY YOU NEED TO RETIRE

CHASING HOT STOCK TOO LATE

INFLEXIBLE STRATEGY

USING WHAT YOU EARN

If you withdraw from your nest egg at the same annual rate at which it's growing, it will stay about the same size. Or, you can gradually reduce the amount to zero by withdrawing at more than the growth rate.

The money you start with	Amount you can withdraw monthly for the number of years below, reducing your nest egg to zero			
	10 years	15 years	20 years	30 years
$50,000	$580	$448	$386	$332
$100,000	$1,160	$896	$772	$668
$150,000	$1,740	$1,340	$1,160	$999
$200,000	$2,320	$1,790	$1,550	$1,330
$250,000	$2,900	$2,240	$1,930	$1,660
$300,000	$3,480	$2,690	$2,320	$1,990
$350,000	$4,060	$3,138	$2,706	$2,322

Based on 7% interest, compounded monthly

The Right Moves

To earn more with your investments, consider what they cost as well as what they pay.

You can use a number of basic investing techniques to help you build your long-term investment portfolio. Of course, they can't guarantee the results you'll achieve. But they can provide a framework for making decisions.

DOLLAR COST AVERAGING

The old adage that the smartest way to make money is to buy at the lowest price and sell at the highest is easier to say than it is to accomplish. If you could do that regularly, funding your retirement—or anything else—would be no problem.

A less dramatic but more reliable strategy is to make monthly or quarterly investments in specific mutual funds. It's much easier to spread your investment over a year rather than to come up with the amount all at once. And over time you can build a substantial account.

Using this approach, called **dollar cost averaging**, you may be able to lower the overall cost of your investment. Since mutual fund prices fluctuate, sometimes you'll buy at a higher price, sometimes at a lower one. When the price is low, your $100 buys more. When it's high, it buys less. You don't risk making a major investment just before a major drop in price. But you have to invest when prices drop as well as when they're up for this strategy to work. Of course, dollar cost averaging does not guarantee a profit or protect against loss in declining markets.

To use dollar cost averaging for stock purchases, you can enroll in a company-sponsored reinvestment plan that lets you make additional purchases. Many larger companies offer this option. Or you can put a regular amount each month in a special investment account.

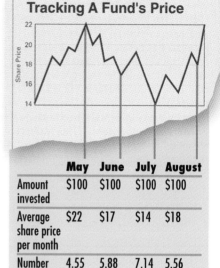

Tracking A Fund's Price

	May	June	July	August
Amount invested	$100	$100	$100	$100
Average share price per month	$22	$17	$14	$18
Number of shares purchased	4.55	5.88	7.14	5.56

AVERAGE SHARE PRICE

$$\frac{\text{Average price per month}}{\text{Number of months}} = \text{Average share price}$$

for example

$$\frac{(\$22 + 17 + 14 + 18)}{4} = \$17.75$$

AVERAGE SHARE COST

$$\frac{\text{Total amount invested}}{\text{Total shares purchased}} = \text{Average share cost}$$

for example

$$\frac{\$400}{4.55 + 5.88 + 7.14 + 5.56} = \$17.29$$

If you have no trouble sticking to a buying schedule, you can write the checks yourself. The advantage is more flexibility, letting you change the amount or skip an occasional month. Or, if it's more convenient, you can arrange for automatic deposits into your account.

INVESTING STYLES

When you **buy and hold**, you keep a stock or bond for the long term. Or you can **trade**, by turning over your portfolio regularly, buying when you think a stock is going to increase in value, and selling when its return meets your expectations.

You might stick to one approach, or use one method for part of your portfolio and the other method for rest. There is a greater risk for big losses, though, if you try to time the market by buying and selling frequently.

AVOIDING THE TAX MAN

Of the two great myths about retirement— that your living expenses will drop dramatically and that you'll owe less income tax—the second is probably the bigger misconception. There's not much you can do to influence the tax rate. But some investing strategies may reduce the income tax you owe— though you may find yourself subject to the **alternative minimum tax (AMT)**. If you're in one of the higher federal tax brackets and live in a high-tax state, one solution is to do some of your investing in tax-exempt municipal bonds. None of the interest is taxed (though **capital gains**, or any profit you make when you sell, will be taxed).

Tax-exempt investments usually pay less interest than taxable investments. You can use the following steps to figure out what you need to earn on a taxable investment to equal the income on a tax-exempt one.

1 Subtract your current **federal tax bracket** from 100. For example, if you're in the 35% bracket, you get 65.

$$100 - 35 = 65$$

2 Divide the yield on the tax-exempt investment by the number you get in step 1. The answer is the taxable yield you need on a taxable investment to equal the tax-exempt yield.

$$\frac{\text{Tax-exempt yield}}{100 - \text{your tax rate}} = \text{Equivalent taxable yield}$$

If you are in the 35% tax bracket, you'd need a taxable yield of 9.2% to earn as much as a tax-exempt investment paying 6%.

for example

$$\frac{6}{65} = .09230$$

**9.2%
THE TAXABLE EQUIVALENT YOU NEED**

BUILDING A LADDER

If you're buying bonds or CDs, you can use a technique known as **laddering**. When you ladder, you choose investments with different maturity dates, and split your total investment more or less equally among the different bonds.

As each bond **matures**, or comes due, you have the principal to reinvest in a new one. If interest rates have dropped, say two percentage points on medium-term bonds, only that part of your total bond investment has to be reinvested at the lower rate. By the time the next bond matures, rates could be up again.

Laddering, in other words, is a way to keep your investments fluid and at the same time protect yourself against having to invest all your money at once if rates are low. Laddered investments can also be used as a regular source of income. As they come due, you can put the money into more liquid accounts to use for living expenses. By planning those cash infusions, you can avoid having to sell off other investments that would continue to produce income, like stocks, longer-term bonds, or mutual funds.

HOW LADDERING WORKS

Purchase three Treasury bonds with varying terms to split up your principal. When each bond matures, re-invest the principal in another bond.

- If interest rates rise, you're able to take advantage of high-yielding investments
- If interest rates drop, you'll have to reinvest only one-third of your total principal at lower rates

Matures 2002
Matures 2005
Matures 2008
Matures 2012
Matures 2015
Matures 2118

BOND 1
BOND 2
BOND 3

Diversification

If variety is the spice of life, diversification is the heart and soul of investing.

While some of your investments are living up to expectations, others may be in the dumps. If you want your **portfolio**, or list of investment holdings, to provide the return you need to meet your long-term goals, you have to **diversify**, or spread your investment money around.

That's because any time all of your money is concentrated in one place, your financial security depends on the strength of that investment. And no matter how sound an investment may be, there will be times when its price falls or its interest payments don't keep up with inflation.

For example, if your life savings are in CDs paying 3% while inflation is running at 4%, you're facing a loss of buying power. Or if you own hundreds of shares in a company that loses money, cuts its dividend, and drops in price, you'll be short dividend income and even part of your original investment if you sell your shares.

THE FIRST STEPS

Diversifying your investments is no easy matter. For starters, you need enough money to make a variety of investments. And you have to judge each one not only on its own merits, but in relation to the rest of your portfolio.

If you put long-term investment money into **fixed-income investments** like corporate or municipal bonds, you should also make **equity investments** like stocks or stock mutual funds. If some of your short-term investments are certificates of deposit (CDs), the rest could be money market funds or U.S. Treasury bills.

THE SECOND STAGE

Diversification also means spreading your investment dollar within a specific type of investment. For example, your stock portfolio is not diversified if you own shares in just one or two companies, or in companies that operate in the same sector of the economy, like healthcare or utility companies. Nor are your fixed-

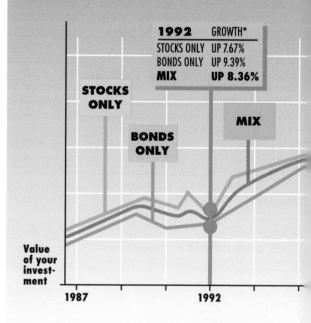

HOW DIVERSIFYING CAN BALANCE GROWTH OVER TIME

1992	GROWTH*
STOCKS ONLY	UP 7.67%
BONDS ONLY	UP 9.39%
MIX	**UP 8.36%**

STOCKS ONLY

BONDS ONLY

MIX

Value of your investment

1987   1992

income investments diversified if you own only municipal bonds issued by the state in which you live. If you invest in three mutual funds, but they all track small-growth companies, you're not diversified either.

Increasingly, real diversification calls for international investments. Because the world economies remain distinct, although they are linked by round-the-clock trading, many investors—and their professional advisers—believe that putting money into overseas markets is a good way to balance investments at home. Generally, buying mutual funds or American Depositary Receipts (ADRs) provides the simplest way to invest internationally, since you don't have to handle the currency and taxation issues that go along with buying and selling abroad.

THE VALUE OF MUTUAL FUNDS

One of the reasons mutual funds keep cropping up in discussions of diversification is that they are, by definition, diversified. A fund may own hundreds of stocks, bonds and other investments. That way, if some of the holdings aren't performing well, they may be offset by others that are doing better. In fact, some funds balance stocks and bonds to provide diversification in different categories of investment and within each of those categories.

Because a fund has so much money to invest, it can achieve a breadth of diversification that no individual can. And because a fund buys and sells in such volume, the cost of diversifying is minimized as well.

ONE MORE THING TO REMEMBER

Diversification is essential for retirement investments. It's especially important if a stock purchase plan is part of your pension plan, because your long-term return will depend on how well that stock does. You'll probably want to balance your dependence on the company's financial health with different investments in your own accounts, including your 401(k) or similar plan.

Diversification is especially important if your company's stock is **cyclical**, that is, a stock strongly influenced by economic conditions. Airline stocks, for example, tend to be depressed in a slow economy because people travel less. If that's the case, you may not want to put too much money into other stocks that behave the same way.

To extend the idea one step further, you may want to think twice about building a portfolio full of stocks and bonds in companies that are in the same business your employer is in. If the pharmaceutical business declines, for example, and all you own are drug company stocks, you'll really need an aspirin.

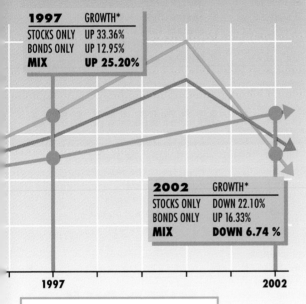

This simplified chart illustrates the advantages of diversifying your portfolio, in this case by investing 60% in stocks and 40% in bonds. While its total value increased less than the better-performing investment in any year, it never did as poorly as the weaker one.

1997	GROWTH*
STOCKS ONLY	UP 33.36%
BONDS ONLY	UP 12.95%
MIX	**UP 25.20%**

2002	GROWTH*
STOCKS ONLY	DOWN 22.10%
BONDS ONLY	UP 16.33%
MIX	**DOWN 6.74 %**

1997   2002

ASK YOURSELF

Diversification isn't a one-shot deal. In analyzing your portfolio, ask the following questions to measure where you are and what's next:

1. What resources have I committed to buying stocks, bonds, mutual funds, real estate, and other money-producing investments?

2. What are those investments worth in relation to each other? How about in comparison to last year? Five years ago? Ten years ago?

3. What investments have I made lately? Are they all basically the same?

4. What am I going to buy next? Why?

DIVERSIFY FOR THE LONG HAUL

Diversifying isn't the same as buying randomly. If anything, it's the opposite, because it means buying according to your strategic plan to get the right mix of growth and income in your investments. But there's nothing wrong with diversifying gradually. If you decide to expand your equity holdings because the stock market seems poised for steady growth, you can do it and think about beefing up your bond portfolio in the months or years ahead.

Investment Risk

There's no such thing as a totally safe investment, but you can choose the level of risk you're comfortable with.

When you invest, you always take a certain amount of risk. At the very worst, you could lose all the money you commit and owe more on top of that. That can be the case with futures contracts or speculative ventures. Or, your **return on investment**—what you get back for what you put in—could be so small it doesn't really count as an investment at all. At the very best, you could invest a small amount in a young company and make a fortune. And between those extremes you have enormous investing choice.

Before you invest, you have to know what the potential risks are as well as your own level of tolerance. If a falling stock market makes you lose sleep or, worse yet, sell in a panic, stocks are probably not the investment for you. On the other hand, investing too conservatively poses the real risk of not earning enough to beat inflation.

ESTIMATING RISK

There's no way to predict how investments will perform in the future or the risks that may limit their return. But by looking at the way that an investment or category of investment has performed in the past, you can get a sense of the level of return it's reasonable to expect.

For example, if the average return on large company stocks has averaged 11% over the past 75 years, it's unrealistic to assume that future returns will average 20% or more, despite the fact that they have been that high or higher in individual years. In other years, they've also been significantly lower.

KEEPING YOUR EYES CLOSED

One of the worst mistakes you can make as an investor is to ignore or minimize the risks you're taking, or to assume that nothing bad is going to happen. By recognizing that volatile investments, like futures, can cost you even more money than you originally put in, you might decide not to try your hand at them. Or, you might limit what you're willing to put into speculative investments to 10% or less.

You also have to be alert to investment advisers who swear that anything is risk-free. It's probably fair to say that the more they promise, the greater the risk they're asking you to take.

THE INVESTMENT PYRAMID

Risk is the result of **volatility** — how much and how quickly the value of an investment changes — and **uncertainty**.

HIGH RISK

- Futures, options, and other derivatives
- Speculative stocks and mutual funds
- Low-rated bonds
- Mining, precious metals

MODERATE RISK

- Growth stocks
- Small company stocks
- Medium-rated corporate, municipal, and zero-coupon bonds
- Growth mutual funds
- Rental real estate

LIMITED RISK

- Blue chip stocks
- High-rated corporate, municipal, and zero-coupon bonds
- Conservative mutual funds
- U.S. Treasury bonds and notes

LOW RISK

- Savings accounts
- Money market accounts and money market funds
- CDs
- U.S. Treasury bills
- Fixed annuities

THE SECURITY OF INSURANCE

One of the reasons people feel comfortable about putting money into bank products—like CDs, money market accounts, and regular savings—is that their investments are insured through the **Federal Deposit Insurance Corporation (FDIC)**. If the bank folds, the money is safe.

Unfortunately, it's not that simple. If a bank is bought out by another bank—a common phenomenon as large regional banks expand—the money will be safe, but the rates depositors had been earning might not be. Banks that acquire others are under no obligation to pay the same CD rates, for example, that the bank they bought paid.

> ### HIGHEST GAINS OR LOSSES
> You can win big, but lose bigger, with risky investments.

Equally important is understanding how much insurance the FDIC provides. Basically, it insures you up to $100,000 per **account category** in each bank. The five categories that most people use are individual, joint, trust, retirement and business accounts. For example, if you had an individual account and an IRA, each of them would be covered up to $100,000. But if you had the same $200,000 in two individual accounts, only $100,000 would be covered. Accounts in separate branches of the same bank are considered one account, but if you have individual accounts in two banks, both are covered.

THE RISK OF HIGH YIELDS

One cardinal rule for successful investing is to know what you're doing. When the economy is down, and interest earnings decline, you might be tempted to seek an investment that produces the same high returns to which you've grown accustomed. The risk is buying lower quality investments (which pay more to attract buyers), or investments you don't know anything about.

> ### LOWEST GAINS OR LOSSES
> $10,000 in a savings account at rates below inflation will be safe but will lose value over time.

Derivative products like collateralized mortgage obligations (CMOs), for example, are often hard to understand and riskier than they seem, despite the promise of a high yield and the comfort of a familiar sounding word: mortgage.

PLAYING IT TOO SAFE

You won't lose your shirt with low-risk investments. But you might not earn enough from them to buy a new shirt when your old one wears out. Trying to avoid risk by investing in only the safest products is a mistake, especially if your retirement is a long way off. If that's your current approach, though, you're not alone. Lots of Americans have most of their retirement money in investments that aren't beating inflation.

The solution is to diversify your risk, just as you diversify the types of investments you make.

OTHER KINDS OF RISK

Beyond the risks of the investments themselves — for example, a new company that fails or an established company that suffers severe losses — there are other risks you can't predict or control but must be prepared for:

MARKET RISK depends on the state of the economy as a whole. If the stock market tumbles, your stock investment will probably decline in value even if the company whose stock you own is making money.

CURRENCY FLUCTUATION is increasingly a factor in investment risk, as more people put money into international markets, especially in mutual funds. As the dollar rises in value, for example, the value of overseas investments declines — and vice versa.

INFLATION RISK affects the value of fixed rate investments like bonds and CDs. If you buy when inflation and interest rates are low, the value of your investments declines as inflation rises because the interest rate isn't adjusted to keep pace.

POLITICAL TURMOIL is a risk because the economies of different nations are closely intertwined. Threats to the oil supply, for example, have disrupted the economy before and could again.

Allocating Your Assets

The recipe for making the most of your investments calls for measuring your ingredients carefully.

One strategic approach to investing is to buy a particular mix of investments that you believe will provide the return you're seeking at a level of risk that you're willing to take. The process of creating such a portfolio is known as **asset allocation**.

The reason that asset allocation can help is that each **asset class**, or investment category, tends to perform differently in different economic conditions. For example, when stocks are providing a strong return, bond returns often slump. And when investors are buying bonds, stock prices tend to slide.

If you're invested in both stocks and bonds over a period of time, you'll be in a better position to avoid the level of loss you'd suffer in a stock downturn if you owned only stocks, or in a bond downturn if you owned only bonds.

STOCKS 60%

BONDS 30%

CASH 10%

TODAY'S SPECIAL

CHOOSE YOUR ALLOCATION STYLE

KEEPING RECORDS

One complication of a diversified portfolio is keeping track of your investments. If simplicity were your primary goal, you could just keep everything in one savings account. You'd never have to wonder about what your investment was worth or where your money was—although you would have to worry about what you were going to live on as inflation eroded the value of your account.

One hands-off approach that does work is to use one financial institution—a brokerage firm, fund company, or bank—for all your investments so you get a consolidated statement each month, detailing your assets and the value of your portfolio. The only extra recordkeeping will be filing confirmations of what you buy and sell so that you can figure your profit or loss for income tax purposes.

If you're like many investors, with a diversity of accounts as well as a diversified portfolio, you'll need to set aside space and time to keep track of your investments.

What you really want to know is how well each one is doing and what portion of your portfolio it makes up.

FORM 1099

FORM K-1

BROKERAGE STATEMENT

ALLOCATION MODELS

Asset allocation plans, or models, tend to focus, for the most part, on securities—stocks and bonds and the mutual funds that invest in stocks and bonds, plus cash or its equivalents—investments which can be easily liquidated, like CDs and U.S. Treasury bills.

The basic approach is to assign a percentage of your total assets to two or more of these asset classes, or investment categories. There are some standard models—such as 60% stock, 30% bond, 10% cash—that many pension funds use to produce the assets they need to meet their obligations to retired workers. Other models, which may emphasize other asset classes or include investments such as real estate, futures and options, or precious metals, are designed to help achieve certain goals or reflect different tolerances for risk.

In addition, brokerage firms and other financial advisers regularly revise and refine the allocation models they suggest to their clients to take current economic conditions into account.

Asset allocation models are important for the personal investments you make outside of a qualified retirement plan as well as for the money you have in a 401(k) or 403(b) plan. You should develop a sense of how much of your total nest egg you want to allocate to each category, and then buy and sell to keep that approximate balance.

Experts maintain that asset allocation accounts for about 90% of the results you get as an investor. Being invested in each of the assets classes means that the class producing stronger returns can help to balance the ones that are faltering at any given time.

AVERAGE INVESTMENT RETURNS 1926-2003

10.4% FOR STOCKS

5.9% FOR BONDS

3.7% FOR CASH

WHAT A DIFFERENCE AN ALLOCATION MAKES

This illustration shows the impact of asset allocation on a hypothetical $100,000 portfolio allocated three different ways.

A one-year return for each allocation was figured using the average return for three asset classes—10.4% for large company stocks, 5.9% for corporate bonds, and 3.7% for cash—for the period 1926-2003, as calculated by Ibbotson Associates. Remember, though, that past performance does not guarantee future results.

60% stock 30% bond 10% cash	OR	30% stock 60% bond 10% cash	OR	10% stock 30% bond 60% cash
$8,380 return		**$7,030 return**		**$5,030 return**

HELP FROM THE COMPUTER

There are a growing number of computer programs and investment websites to help you analyze your investments and keep track of how they're performing. Some are comprehensive tools that incorporate advice with background information and work charts. Mutual fund companies and brokerage firms are typical sources. So are companies whose websites specialize in a specific area, such as retirement planning.

You can get reviews of what's available, plus critiques of how effective they

are, and how complicated they are to use, regularly in personal finance magazines and the business section of many newspapers.

Investment Tracking Software

Asset Allocation Choices

You don't have to reinvent the wheel to plan your asset allocation. It's already been done.

Fortunately, there are a limited number of ways to split up your assets. If you're a cautious investor, you'll stress bonds and cash. And the more aggressive you are—about investing anyway—the more you'll put into stocks. You might even decide that a small percentage of your assets belong in higher-risk investments, like futures or initial public offerings (IPOs).

CASH IN THE BANK

A cash investment is money you can get your hands on in a hurry—like a money market fund—without risking a big loss in value. For example, while putting your money in a regular savings account has serious limitations as an investment strategy, the logic behind a cash reserve makes a lot of sense. If all your assets are tied up in stocks and long-term bonds, and you need to **liquidate**, or turn them to cash quickly, you may take a loss if the market is down. Or, you might miss a great opportunity for new investing.

TAKING STOCK

In an asset allocation model, stocks represent growth. While some stocks pay dividends that provide a regular income, stocks are essential to long-term investment planning because historically they

LOOKING AHEAD

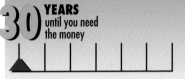

30 YEARS until you need the money

12 YEARS until you need the money

5 YEARS until you need the money

increase in value. While it's possible to lose a lot of money in the stock market in any one year, the longer you stay in the market, the more apt you are to come out ahead.

Financial experts may recommend that you have as much as 80% of your total portfolio in stocks (or stock mutual funds) while you're in your 20s and 30s. That means every time you invest $1,000, $800 of it would go into stocks or stock mutual funds. However, as you get older, say in your 50s and 60s, the percentage of stocks in your portfolio is usually scaled back to 60% or sometimes less. Generally the greater the risk a particular stock carries, the more suitable it is for younger investors or those with substantial assets elsewhere.

STASHING THE CASH

Option	Advantages
Bank money market account	<ul><li>Instant access</li><li>Better interest than savings account</li><li>May reduce cost of checking account</li><li>Check-writing privileges</li><li>FDIC insured</li></ul>
Money market mutual fund	<ul><li>Easy access</li><li>Interest usually higher than bank money market account</li><li>Check-writing privileges</li><li>Some funds offer insurance</li></ul>
CDs	<ul><li>Money available (with early withdrawal penalty possible)</li><li>Interest rate slightly higher than money market accounts</li><li>Due dates can be staggered for convenience</li><li>Bank CDs FDIC insured</li></ul>
U.S. Treasury bills	<ul><li>Short-term investments</li><li>Enough interest to protect against inflation</li><li>Can be sold any time, though at a potential loss</li><li>Extremely safe</li></ul>

INVESTING

**SHIFTING GEARS
FOR SHIFTING GOALS**
As retirement gets closer you might want to shift
your assets from seeking growth toward income.

STOCKS	BONDS	CASH
80% Aggresive growth funds Small company stocks Blue-chip stocks	**15%** Long-term bonds High-yield municipal bond fund	**5%** Money market account
60% Blue chip stocks Small company stocks S&P index fund	**30%** Zero coupon bonds Intermediate bonds	**10%** Money market account CD
40% Blue chip stocks Growth and income or equity income fund	**40%** U.S. Treasury notes Municipal bonds	**20%** CD Money market account Treasury bills

THE BOND'S THE THING

Bonds have traditionally been seen as income-producing investments. In that case, you buy a bond, hold it to maturity and receive a regular interest payment every six months or year. Then you get the principal back when the bond matures. As an added plus, bonds issued by the U.S. government are virtually safe from **default,** or failure to pay what's due. That's one reason these bonds appeal to investors—often those nearing retirement—who are looking for steady income and don't want to risk losing their investment.

Most experts advise all investors to include bonds—or bond mutual funds—in their portfolios because they provide additional diversification and can help reduce the overall volatility of your portfolio. Advisers say stashing part of your holdings in a diverse basket of bonds can serve as a financial shock absorber. For example, you might buy some mix of government, corporate and municipal bonds of different maturities. Just remember, though, that prices of long-term bonds, especially zero-coupon bonds, can sometimes be highly volatile themselves.

OTHER FIXED INCOME

Corporate and government bonds are the best known, but not the only, fixed income investments. Mortgage-based investments like relatively conservative **Ginnie Maes,** sold by the Government National Mortgage Association, as well as the riskier **CMOs,** or collateralized mortgage obligations, which derive from a package of mortgages, repay your investment with interest. But what you get back often depends more on the state of the economy than it does with corporate or government bonds. For example, if interest rates drop and lots of people refinance their mortgages, investments based on mortgages reflect the amounts being paid back and the rates at which the new loans are made.

Certain fixed or variable annuity contracts also provide regular income, usually after you retire. Unlike bonds, with their established maturity dates, the return is paid out either over your lifetime, or for a period you and the issuer agree on.

GINNIE MAE

CMO

Figuring Yield

One way to measure how well your investments are doing is to look at what they're paying.

Choosing the right mix of investments is only half the battle. To know if you're succeeding—that is, if your investments are really performing well—you need to know how to measure the **yield** and the **return** your investments provide.

U.S. EXCHANGE BONDS

NET CHG.	BONDS	CUR YLD.	VOL.	CLOSE	NET CHG.
+ ⅝	DevonE 4.95s08	cv	50	102	+ ¼
+ ½	Dole 7s03	7.0	25	100¼	– 1
– ⅜	Dole 7⅞13	8.1	106	97⅛	– ⅜
– ¼	DukeEn 6⅜08	6.3	15	101¼	+ ⅝
– 2⅜	DukeEn 6¾25	7.0	13	96½	...
+ ¼	DukeEn 7½25	7.3	15	103½	+ ⅜
+ ⅛	DukeEn 7s33	7.0	67	99¼	+ ⅛
+ 1⅛	FnclFed 4½05	cv	3	96	– 5
– ⅞	Florsh 12¾02	25.3	10	50½	...
– ⅜	FordCr 6⅜08	6.4	25	100¼	...
+ ⅛	GBCB 8⅜07	8.7	1	96	+ ⅜
+ 3⅞	GEICap 7⅞06	7.0	88	111¾	– ⅝
– 1¼	GMA 5½01	5.5	43	99 27/32	– 5/32
+ ⅛	GMA 6⅝02	6.5	2	101¾	+ ¼
– ¼	GMA 8¾05	8.0	9	110	– ¼
– ¼		6.3	25		

BONDS	CUR YLD.	VOL.	CLOSE	NET CHG.
IBM 6.45s07	6.2	105	104¼	+ ⅝
IBM 6½28	6.7	20	97	+ ½
JPMChse 6½09	6.4	3	102⅛	– ⅜
K&B Hm 9⅜03	9.3	72	101¼	– ¼
Loews 3⅛07	cv	48	84⅛	– 2⅜
LglsLt 8.2s23	7.9	121	103¼	+ ¼
Lucent 7¼06	9.0	1234	80⅜	+ ⅛
Lucent 5½08	7.9	160	69⅝	+ 1⅛
Lucent 6½28	9.9	47	66	– ⅞
Lucent 6.45s29	10.1	504	63⅝	– ⅜
MBNA 8.28s26	8.5	45	98	+ ⅛
MSC Sf 7⅞04	cv	258	124	+ 3⅞
Malan 9½04	cv	40	93¾	– 1¼
MarO 7s02	7.0	42	100 13/32	+ ⅛
Mascotch 03	cv	44	80½	– ¼
MKT 5½33f	...	232	99	– ¼
	4.6	10	93	+

LOOKING FOR YIELD

You find yield by dividing what you receive in interest or dividends on an investment by the amount you spent for it.

for example

$	100	Annual interest
÷	2,000	Invested
=	5%	**YIELD**

Current yield is usually different from the interest rate a bond investment pays although both are stated as a percentage of the par value.

While current yield depends on the rate, it represents what someone paying the current price of the bond, rather than its stated, or par, value, receives on the investment. When the price is more than par, the yield is lower than the interest rate, and when the price is less, the rate is higher.

For example, the JP Morgan Chase bond paying 6½ (6.5%) interest is currently

COMPOUNDING YIELD

The yield on CDs depends on the frequency with which the interest is **compounded**, or paid. A CD with a simple interest rate of 5%, added once a year, yields 5%, or $50 on a $1,000 investment. But if the rate is compounded, meaning it's added to your balance daily, weekly or monthly, the yield will be higher. The more frequently it's compounded, the greater the yield. For example, a compounded rate of 5.11% would yield 5.25%, or $52.50 on $1,000.

avings Ba
Money Market Rate!
3.00
ANNUAL PERCENTAGE YIELD%
2.9
INTEREST RATE%
PLUS CDs!
TWO YEAR CD
5.25
ANNUAL PERCENTAGE YIELD%
5.1
INTEREST RATE%
SIX MONTH CD
4.90
ANNUAL PERCENTAGE YIELD%
4.78
INTEREST RATE%
For more information and current rates on all our
and accounts, stop by your local bran
Customer Information Cent

ANOTHER VIEW OF BONDS

Bonds lead a double life in the current investment world. In their traditional role as income producers, they're the backbone of conservative investment portfolios: For little risk and less bother, you get a steady return. However, bond prices and their yields fluctuate in response to changing economic conditions. A strong **secondary market**, where bonds are bought and sold, flourishes, and many investors buy bonds to trade. That means the old rule of buying low and selling high applies. However, the commissions on bond trading can be high. To trade bonds, you also need substantial amounts of money to make the small price differences pay off, as well as a greater tolerance for risk than is generally associated with buying bonds.

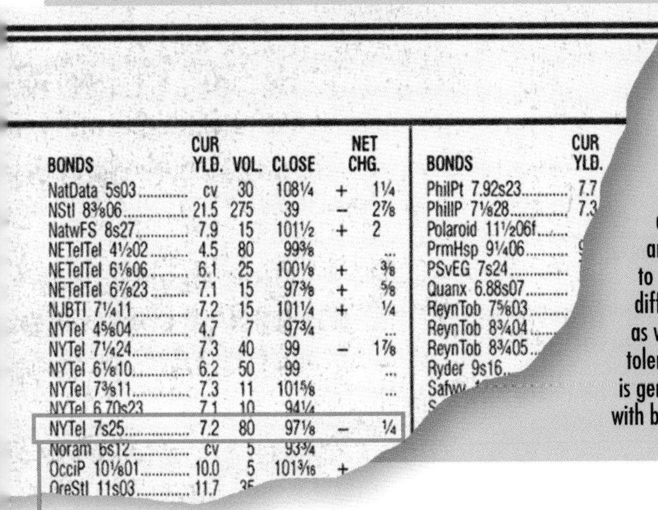

BONDS	CUR YLD.	VOL.	CLOSE	NET CHG.
NatData 5s03	cv	30	108¼	+ 1¼
NStl 8⅜06	21.5	275	39	– 2⅞
NatwFS 8s27	7.9	15	101½	+ 2
NETelTel 4½02	4.5	80	99⅜	...
NETelTel 6⅛06	6.1	25	100⅛	+ ⅜
NETelTel 6⅞23	7.1	15	97⅜	+ ⅝
NJBTl 7¼11	7.2	15	101¼	+ ¼
NYTel 4⅝04	4.7	7	97¾	...
NYTel 7¼24	7.3	40	99	– 1⅞
NYTel 6⅛10	6.2	50	99	...
NYTel 7⅜11	7.3	11	101⅝	...
NYTel 6.70s23	7.1	10	94¼	
NYTel 7s25	7.2	80	97⅛	– ¼
Noram 6s12	cv	5	93¾	
OcciP 10⅛01	10.0	5	101³⁄₁₆	+
OreStl 11s03	11.7	35		

BONDS	CUR YLD.
PhilPt 7.92s23	7.7
PhilIP 7⅛28	7.3
Polaroid 11½06f	
PrmHsp 9¼06	
PSvEG 7s24	
Quanx 6.88s07	
ReynTob 7⅝03	
ReynTob 8¾04	
ReynTob 8¾05	
Ryder 9s16	
Safwy	

yielding 6.4% because the price is $1,021.25 (102⅛), or $21.25 (2⅛) above par. In contrast, the New York Telephone bond paying 7% interest is currently yielding 7.2% because the bond is selling for $971.25 (97⅛), or $29.75 below par.

Also keep in mind that there are several different ways to calculate yields on fixed income investments. For example, there is the yield based on the earliest date a bond may be **called**, or redeemed, by the issuer. And there is **yield to maturity**, or what your total return would be, in today's dollars, if you held the bond until it matured.

So when a salesperson mentions yield, be sure to ask for details.

Blindly seeking yield has some drawbacks. The promise of a higher yield on a riskier investment that you don't really know much about, like a high-yield bond, may not justify switching from a safer and more familiar U. S. Treasury or agency bond. When interest rates are low, this strategy seems appealing. But most experts caution against putting money into investments that you don't understand or that your broker can't explain to your satisfaction.

SHOPPING FOR CD YIELD

It makes sense to find the best yield you can when there's a basis for comparison, like the interest rates on different investments in relation to their liquidity. Unless you're dealing with large sums of money, however, the difference of a quarter percent makes very little difference in your yield, especially on short-term investments like most CDs. If the larger yield is offered by a bank you're unfamiliar with, the inconvenience and potential risk may not be worth the few dollars difference. For example, if your $25,000 CD is yielding 5% in your local bank and 5.25% in a bank you know nothing about half a continent away, the $62.50 difference in earnings may not be worth making the switch.

Timing is also an issue. When interest rates are low, it may not pay to tie up your money in a longer-term CD, for example, that yields only a percentage point or two more than short-term ones. If rates go up, as they invariably do, you risk being locked into a lower yield or facing a loss if you liquidate. One solution may be a CD with an adjustable interest rate, which will increase at least once if rates in general go up.

Finding Return

The real test of success for any investment is what you get back for what you put in.

When you invest for growth, **total return**, or the amount your investment increases in value *plus* the interest or dividends it has paid, is the best measure of how well it has performed.

For example, if you spent $6,000 for stock that's now worth $8,000, and you received $360 in dividends, your total return is $2,360.

$\underline{\begin{array}{lr}
\$ & 2,000 \text{ Gain} \\
+ \$ & 360 \text{ Dividends}
\end{array}}$

$2,360 TOTAL RETURN

You can use the total return to figure the **percent return**, which you can compare with the return on other investments. To find that percentage, you divide the total return by the price you paid for the investment.

$\underline{\begin{array}{lr}
\$ & 2,360 \text{ Total return} \\
\div \$ & 6,000 \text{ Price of investment}
\end{array}}$

39.3 PERCENT RETURN

If you bought and sold the stocks within one year, your annual percent return would be the full 39.3%. But if you'd held the stock three years, for example, the annual percent return would be 13.1%.

COMPARISON PROBLEMS

While it's relatively easy to compare the return on similar investments, such as two mutual funds that buy small company stock, it's much harder to compare your return on different kinds of investments. Here are some of the factors that make comparisons difficult:

Time

The length of time you hold different investments varies, making it hard to assess gain or loss in value for a fixed period. So does the timing of your buys and sells. Buying just before a market dip, for instance, can skew your results downward.

Taxes

You have to consider the impact of taxes on investment return. Long-term capital gains and most dividends are taxed at a lower rate than interest or short-term gains. Interest on some bonds is tax exempt, while interest on other bonds is taxable. And some mutual funds are managed to limit taxable income.

RETURN ON STOCK INVESTMENTS

If you bought 200 shares of Minnesota Mining & Manufacturing stock at a low of 80.50 and sold it at a high of 127, your total return would have been $9,780, or 61%:

$	25,400	Selling price
−	16,100	Purchase price
= $	9,300	Return on transaction
+	480	Dividends at $2.40/share
= $	9,780	**TOTAL RETURN**
÷ $	16,100	Purchase price
=	.6075	**or**
	61	**PERCENT RETURN**

NEW YORK

52 WEEKS				YLD	
HI	LO	STOCK (SYM)	DIV	%	PE
54.06	28.94▲	MinrlTch **MTX**	.10	.2	19
127	80.50	MN MngMfr **MMM**	2.40	2.2	28 1
47.20	20.56	Mirant **MIR** n	...	...	6
5.36	2.43	MS Chem **GRO**			
	28.81	MitchEnr			

Method of figuring return

The performance of an investment can be **averaged** or **compounded**, and the method can make a big difference in the return. To figure average return, you add the return for each of the years in your sample and divide by the total number of years. But in figuring a compound return, you have to weigh the impact of each year's return on the total. For example, a return totalling 27% over three years would be 9% a year if the return were **averaged**, or **annualized**, no matter what each annual return was. But a **compounded** three-year return

MUTUAL FUNDS QUARTERLY REVIEW

FUND NAME	OBJECTIVE	MAX. SALES CHARGE INITIAL	EXIT	ANNUAL EXP AS %	NAV $ 9/28	PERFORMANCE & RANK †ANNUALIZED THIRD QUARTER	YEAR-TO-DATE	ONE YEAR	THREE YEARS†	FIVE YEARS†
Sht Horz Str All	GT	NO	NO	0.20	10.75	1.3	3.7	6.6A	4.7A	5.9B
Stock Index	NA	NO	NO		8.10	pNN	NN	NN	NN	NN
Value & Income	EI	NO	NO	1.00	20.49	p −8.1	−8.5	−1.7A	6.8A	10.8A
Smith & Jones										
Balanced	BL	NO	NO	0.53	62.24	−5.2	1.6	11.1A	12.5A	12.6A
Income	AB	NO	NO	0.46	12.35	4.2	9.7	14.2A	6.7A	8.1A
Stock	XV	NO	NO	0.54	91.48	−10.2	−2.8	8.6A	15.5A	14
Stewart Soc Inv										
Inst Social Equity	LC	NO	NO	0.33	15.88	−14.1	−20.5			

On the other hand, if you bought high and sold low, your return could be a loss, despite earning the same dividends earnings of $480.

In any case, you have to figure total return for yourself. That number doesn't appear in the daily stock exchange columns.

RETURN ON MUTUAL FUNDS

A mutual fund's return, reported as **performance** and shown as a percentage, is tracked over different time periods. This quarterly review reports returns for the quarter, the year-to-date, and one, three, and five years. A gain is indicated by a + before the percentage, while a – indicates a loss.

For example, the Smith & Jones Stock fund has a negative return for the quarter and the year to date, but positive returns over the longer periods. Results for longer than one year are annualized.

Smith & Jones Balanced fund has a year-to-date return of 1.6%, a stronger 11.1% for one year and 12.6% annualized over the last five years.

STOCK EXCHANGE

NET CHG	52 WEEKS HI	LO	STOCK (SYM)	DIV	YLD %	PE	VOL 100S
+ 0.43	13.06	7.26	MitsuTokyo ADR **MTF**	.08e	1.1	...	2191
+ 3.30	32	21.25	MobilTelesys **MBT**		...	...	10
+ 0.26	8	3.38	ModisProSvc **MPS**		...	6	1
+ 0.16	42.94	19.06	MohawkInd **MHK**				

could reflect an initial bad year offset by a final good one.

Investment purpose

If you have money in real estate, limited partnerships, and other investments that are hard to put a current value on or difficult to **liquidate** by turning them into cash, you can't figure return the same way or make a meaningful comparison. But many of these investments have tax advantages that aren't reflected in return and are the real motive for buying them in the first place.

APPLES AND ORANGES

While comparison can be hard, it's certainly not impossible if you're thinking in terms of stocks, bonds, and mutual funds. For example, if you want to compare a stock investment to a bond investment, you have to find the **annual return** on each one, or what you've made each year, as a percentage of your investment. For example, if you compare a bond yielding 8% to a stock with a dividend yield of 2% but a total return of 12.8%, you determine that the stock performance is stronger.

The comparison between stocks and bonds (or between stock mutual funds and bond mutual funds) is more telling when you compare stocks to riskier bonds and other high-yielding investments. The likelihood that the riskier bond will continue to pay well over the long haul—the time frame of investing for retirement—is small. Plus, you face at least as great a risk of losing your principal with these bonds as you do with stocks, and in some cases significantly more risk.

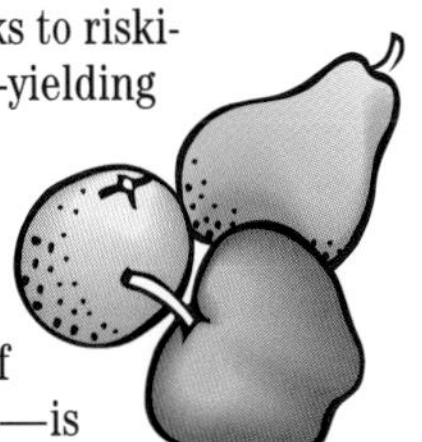

However, given the different goals of your investments, the most meaningful comparisons are those that compare similar investments, or investments with similar goals, like growth or income production.

Deferred Annuities

Annuities are appealing because they grow tax-deferred.

A deferred annuity is a contract you make with an insurance company. You invest money, either as a lump sum or over a period of years, building up a pool of income you can tap after you retire. The insurance company administers the contract, and pays out your benefit either as a lump sum or a series of payments. Because annuities are retirement plans, your investment grows tax deferred, increasing the rate at which your earnings are able to accumulate.

A fixed annuity is a contract you make with an insurance company.

THE INVESTOR

"I agree to invest a set amount in the annuity, either in a lump sum or over a period of years."

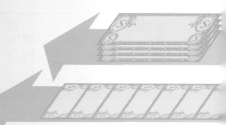

Your money grows tax deferred

FIXED OR VARIABLE

If you choose a deferred annuity, you'll have to choose between a fixed or a variable account. A **fixed annuity** is the more conservative choice. It promises a set rate of return, though the rate can be—and usually is—reset regularly. In many cases, the initial rate, or the one you're quoted when you buy your annuity, is higher than the rate at which your investment will actually grow.

If the rates drop, the earnings that have been projected for your investment decline—sometimes quite dramatically. While most fixed annuities have a **floor**, or guarantee of a minimum rate, it can be as low as current bank savings rates.

Unlike a fixed annuity, a **variable annuity** lets you choose how your money is invested. The selection of subaccounts, typically mutual funds, may be limited, and the return is not guaranteed. But you can put your money into higher paying investments than a fixed annuity, and you can profit by putting what you know to work for your own benefit. In that way, you can compare a variable annuity with a 401(k). In each case, you're responsible for deciding how your retirement savings will be invested. A major difference, though, is that the money you invest in annuities has already been taxed.

Advocates of variable annuities point out that a number of new products are being introduced that let you combine the assurance of a steady long-term income with the opportunity to put money into investments likely to produce strong returns. In addition, as an increasing number of providers offer annuities, many have responded to the competition by lowering their fees.

Though finding an annuity that gives you the kind of return on investment you want may take some work, it can be worth the search.

COLLECTING ON YOUR ANNUITY

After the **accumulation** phase, when your annuity investment grows, there comes a point when you start collecting—and paying the taxes you've deferred.

You can choose among **annuitizing**, which means receiving lifetime payouts based on your contract, using the money to buy an immediate annuity from another source, or taking a lump sum withdrawal.

If you're taking the regular payments, you owe tax on the earnings portion of each payout, a calculation that the company will provide. If you take a lump sum, though, you owe all the tax that's due up front, since you can't roll the amount over into an IRA so you can continue to defer taxes. Those taxes are figured at your regular income tax rate.

You can usually take money out of your annuity sporadically. If you're over 59½, there's no penalty, but you may get stuck with an extra tax bill if the IRS says that the entire withdrawal is made up of earnings, not principal. It's also possible to begin regular withdrawals before you retire, taking up to 10% of the total value of your account each year. Then you owe tax on the earnings portion only.

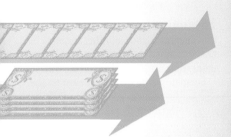

You have a source of retirement income

THE INSURANCE COMPANY

"We agree to pay a benefit based on the plan's earnings, beginning at an agreed retirement date."

DEFERRED ANNUITIES—THE PROS AND CONS

Deferred annuities, both fixed and variable, provide major investment benefits. For all their charms, however, deferred annuities also have some drawbacks.

ADVANTAGES	DRAWBACKS
● **Tax-deferred growth**	● **Penalties if you withdraw early, or in some cases, if you make a lump sum withdrawal**
● **No limit on the amount you can contribute each year**	● **Minimized tax advantages for high-income tax payers because earnings are taxed as straight income, not at lower capital gains rate**
● **No mandatory withdrawals when you reach age 70½**	
● **A wide choice of plans, letting you find one that suits your investing style and goals**	● **Potentially large fees, which reduce investment growth, a particular problem with variable annuities**

A side benefit of receiving annuity income is that the part that's return of principal doesn't count when you're figuring out whether part of your Social Security is taxable. Unlike income from other investments — including tax-exempt municipal bonds — which you have to add when you figure your annual income, you can ignore this percentage of your annuity income.

● **Lack of liquidity, especially in fixed annuities, though they may grow at a rate similar to cash-equivalent investments, including U.S. Treasurys**

Immediate Annuities

If you buy an immediate annuity, you'll get retirement income on a regular schedule.

Immediate annuities fill a specific niche in retirement planning by providing a regular monthly income, the way a pension annuity does. But instead of building up your assets over time, you buy the annuity with one lump sum premium and usually start collecting right away.

Insurance companies sell the annuities, administer your contract, and with fixed annuities, invest your money. That's a major attraction for many people, who prefer not to be responsible for investment decisions or money management themselves.

Buy an Annuity

Get Paid Monthly

COMPARISON SHOPPING

The amount of your monthly annuity check is based on the size of your investment, your age, and what the insurance company estimates it will earn on the investment you're making. In fact, the monthly payout on the same

sized investment can vary enormously from company to company. So get several different proposals to be sure you end up with the best deal.

You should also look at the financial stability of the insurance company itself. Because you're making a lifetime deal, you want the company to be around to make your payments. Though a high rating from A. M. Best & Company or Standard & Poor's doesn't guarantee a company will stay solvent, a poor rating can spell trouble. Ask your agent, and check the financial press for ratings.

Also be wary of buying an annuity from anyone who wants you to act quickly. That's especially true if you're feeling the stress of making financial decisions or if you're looking for a way to invest a large sum of money, like an inheritance or a capital gain. The only one who benefits from speed is the person who sells the annuity.

MAKING CHOICES

If you do decide on an immediate annuity, you'll have to make some decisions about the terms of the annuity contract. Among other things, an annuity is **irrevocable**, which means you can't change your mind once you've made the purchase. And, there's usually no lump-sum repayment provision. That's why it's especially important to understand some of the basics.

You also have to decide how much to invest. Experts advise no more than 25% of your nest egg.

ARE THEY SMART?

Whether immediate annuities are smart investments depends very much on your personal situation. Among the points to consider are where an immediate annuity fits in your overall retirement plan and if there are better choices for your investment dollars. It might make sense, for example, to roll your pension payout over into a tax-deferred IRA. However, you will have to set up a withdrawal plan on your own.

Without question, one major advantage of an immediate fixed annuity is the security of a guaranteed income. If returns on other investments dip—because interest rates are down or the stock market slumps—annuity payments remain steady. Since you've already paid taxes on the money you use to buy an annuity, typically up to half of the income is tax free.

On the down side, if you buy an annuity when interest rates are down, your payments may not keep up with inflation. And while you aren't responsible for managing your portfolio, that also means you can't take advantage of changing market conditions to make better investments.

For a Certain Amount of Time

SINGLE LIFE ANNUITIES are paid each month for the duration of your lifetime. The advantage of single life is that your payment will be larger than with other lifetime payment options. But when you die, the payments stop. If you have a survivor who is dependent on your annuity income, that could be a problem.

It's also true that if you die within a short time of buying the annuity, you don't get your money's worth. For example, if you invested $50,000 in an annuity that paid you $450 a month, you'd have to live more than nine years to get back what you put in.

LIFE OR PERIOD CERTAIN ANNUITIES are paid for your lifetime or for a fixed period of time. You get less each month than you would with a single life plan, but if you die before the fixed term ends, your beneficiary receives the payments instead. That way, you've protected your investment if you don't live long enough to get it back. Unlike life insurance, though, the amount due to your beneficiary is not paid as a lump sum, but in annuity payments of the same size that you were receiving.

JOINT AND SEVERAL ANNUITIES are paid over your lifetime and the lifetime of your beneficiary, usually your spouse. When things work right, the smaller monthly payments are offset by being paid out over a longer period of time.

The one drawback is if your beneficiary dies shortly after the annuity begins. Since you're getting a smaller payment, you'll have to live longer to recoup your investment.

BUILDING A LADDER

If you're ready to buy an annuity, but interest rates are low, you can divide the amount you've set aside for annuities and buy a series of smaller annuities over four or five years instead of one larger one.

The technique resembles laddering bond or CD investments, and lets you hold back some of your money on the expectation of getting a higher rate down the road. It means cashing several monthly checks instead of one, but if your income is higher, it's probably worth it.

What's Your Estate?

An estate isn't just expensive property surrounded by a fence.

Your estate is everything you own in your own name, and your share of anything you own with other people. Your property can be **real**—meaning land and buildings—or **personal**, such as jewelry, a stamp collection, or a favorite table or chair. Money is property, too, as are stocks and bonds, a mutual fund account, or a life insurance policy.

The actual value of your estate is computed only after you die—when you're not around to figure it out. But realistically, you need

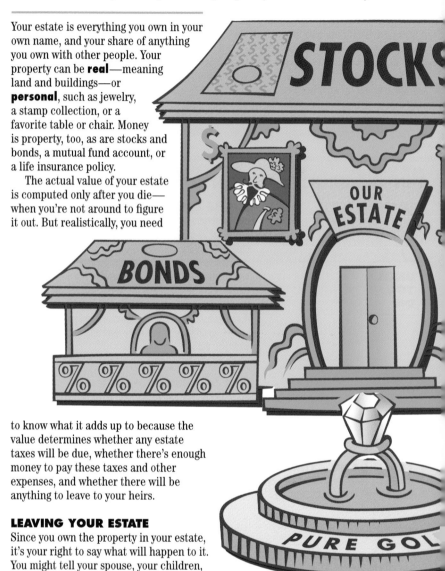

to know what it adds up to because the value determines whether any estate taxes will be due, whether there's enough money to pay these taxes and other expenses, and whether there will be anything to leave to your heirs.

LEAVING YOUR ESTATE

Since you own the property in your estate, it's your right to say what will happen to it. You might tell your spouse, your children, or your lawyer what you want to happen, but unless it's written down, there's no assurance your wishes will be respected.

There are several ways to make clear what you want to happen to your estate.

- You can write a **will** to specify who gets what after you die

- You can create one or more **trusts** to pass property, or income from that property, to others

- You can name **beneficiaries** on pension funds, insurance policies, and other investments so they will receive the payouts directly

- You can own property **jointly** with other people, so that it becomes theirs when you die

Since wills and trusts are legal documents, you should consult your lawyer about them. Naming beneficiaries is simpler, usually requiring only your signature. And owning joint property such as homes and bank accounts—especially with your spouse—is fairly standard.

WHAT'S YOUR ESTATE WORTH?

Finding the value of an estate is a two-step process—adding up what it's worth and then subtracting the expenses of settling it.

Usually, the valuation is figured as of the date of your death. The alternative is to value the estate six months after you die, if waiting will decrease its value and therefore reduce the potential tax.

An estate's worth is figured by finding the **fair market value** of its real and personal property. That's not easy to determine ahead of time, in part because market values change over time, and in part because evaluators may appraise the same property differently.

Just as everything you own is part of your estate, what you owe reduces its value. Your income taxes, mortgages or other debts, funeral expenses, and the costs of settling your estate—which can be substantial—are all

deducted from your estate's assets. So is the value of any property you transfer to a charity or to your surviving spouse. What's left is the value of your estate.

NOT IN YOUR ESTATE?

If you no longer own property, it's out of your estate. Something you give away belongs to the new owner. The same is true of something you sell.

You might owe gift or capital gains taxes on the transfer, but its value isn't included in your estate. The larger your estate, the more important it is to reduce it as much as you can to reduce estate taxes.

SETTING A VALUE

One workable definition of *fair market value* is the amount someone would be willing to pay for your property, and that you'd be willing to accept—assuming that neither one of you is under any pressure to buy or sell, nor guilty of any misrepresentation.

An Estate Inventory

If you own your home, have invested money, and are in a pension plan, the value of your estate is apt to be greater than you think. Here's a checklist of what might be included:

 Real estate

 Securities (stocks, bonds, and mutual funds)

 Interest and dividends you're owed that haven't been paid

 Bank accounts

 All tangible personal property

 Life insurance policies you own

 No-fault insurance payments due to you

 Annuities paid by contract or agreement

 Value of any retirement savings plan, including IRAs

 Claims paid for pain and suffering, even after your death (but not claims for wrongful death)

 Income tax refunds

 Forgiven debts

 Dower and curtesy interests

 UGMA and UTMA custodial accounts for which you are the custodian, if you created the accounts

 Closely held businesses

What's in a Name?

If your estate includes everything you own, you want to be pretty clear about what ownership means.

Most people think of real property when the subject of ownership comes up, but all kinds of property—bank accounts, stocks, mutual funds—can be owned in a variety of ways. The way you own your property determines the flexibility you have to sell it while you're alive, and also what happens to it after you die.

Basically, there are four ways to be a property owner:

- By yourself, as a **sole owner**
- As a **joint owner**
- In an arrangement called **tenants by the entirety**, and
- As **tenants in common**

In addition, if you're married and live in a community property state, half of what you buy or earn during your marriage legally belongs to your spouse.

JT TN W/ROS

This cryptic acronym, which frequently appears on bank accounts and mutual fund statements, stands for **joint tenants with rights of survivorship**. It means that both owners have equal access to the property while they're alive, and the property belongs to the survivor when one of them dies. For example, if you and your mother have a joint checking account with survivorship rights and your mother dies, the money is yours.

ESTATE IMPLICATIONS

If you own property jointly with your spouse and you die first, only half the jointly held property is added to your estate. For example, if you and your husband own a $200,000 house jointly, and you die, only half the value, or $100,000, is counted in figuring the value of your estate.

If the joint owner is someone other than your spouse—such as your child or a friend—the rule is that the entire value of the property is added to the estate of the person who dies first—which is more likely to be you rather than your child. If you owned a $200,000 house jointly with your daughter, for example, the entire $200,000 would be added to your estate at your death—even though she would become sole owner of the house. The only

CERTIFICATE OF TITLE

SOLE OWNERSHIP

- One person
- No limits on right to sell or gift, or pass by will or trust

CERTIFICATE OF TITLE

JOINT TENANTS, WITH RIGHTS OF SURVIVORSHIP

- Two (or, rarely, more) people, often but not always a married couple
- Any owner can sell during his or her lifetime by agreement of all owners, and as long as all owners receive proportional share of profits. Property goes directly to surviving owner(s) when other owner dies, not through will or trust

VOID IF

CERTIFICATE OF TITLE

TENANTS BY THE ENTIRETY

- A married couple
- Neither can sell without the other's permission. Surviving spouse becomes sole owner. In a divorce, former spouses become tenants in common

CERTIFICATE OF TITLE

TENANTS IN COMMON

- Two or more people, each owning a share. The shares are usually equal
- Each owner owns and can sell his or her share independently. Each share can be passed by will or trust. Other owner(s) has no legal interest or right to inherit

VOID IF ALTERED

WHO'S COMPETENT ANYWAY?

Competence, like beauty, may be in the eye of the beholder, but when it comes to decisions about your estate, your competence may have to be legally determined. There's a generally recognized test that's often applied: Do you have a general knowledge of your affairs and do you know "the natural objects of your bounty?" Those "objects" are generally understood to be the members of your family, especially your children, if you have any.

If, for example, you make a will that omits any mention of your children, they might be able to challenge the will in court, on the grounds that forgetting about them shows you weren't competent to decide where your money should go. But if you mention them by name in the will and leave them each a dollar, your competence is not as open to question because you are clearly indicating your intentions.

way to avoid this situation, and the possibility of increased tax on your estate, is to be able to prove the amount that each of you contributed to accumulating the property.

POWER CONTROL

Being a property owner gives you the right to control what happens to that property, at least as long as you are healthy, solvent, and of sound mind. And, of course, it also helps if you're around to keep an eye on it. But what happens if you aren't able to exercise control for one reason or another?

One solution is to grant, or give, **power of attorney** to your spouse, sibling, adult child, or close friend—someone you trust to act wisely and in your best interest. This attorney-in-fact, or agent, has the legal right to make the decisions you would make if you were able, as well as the authority to buy and sell property and to write checks on your accounts.

A lawyer can draw up the power of attorney for you, specifying the authority you are granting, and excluding those things you still want to control. Many experts suggest that you, as **grantor**, or principal, update a power of attorney—or even write

a new one—every four or five years so it will be less vulnerable to legal challenges.

Since an ordinary power of attorney is revoked if you become physically or mentally disabled, you can take the additional step of granting **durable power of attorney**. Unlike a limited or ordinary agreement, durable power is not revoked if you become incompetent, so you're not left in the lurch when you need assistance most. But not all states allow it, so check with your legal adviser.

You can also establish a **springing power of attorney**, which takes effect only at the point that you're unable to act for yourself. In every case but the last, you can revoke the power at any time, or choose a different agent.

A LESSER POWER

Unlike someone with power of attorney, a **payee representative** can receive your income and pay your bills — but nothing more. You still control your other financial affairs. But this arrangement helps you keep your accounts in order if you can't do them yourself because you're ill, traveling, or just too busy.

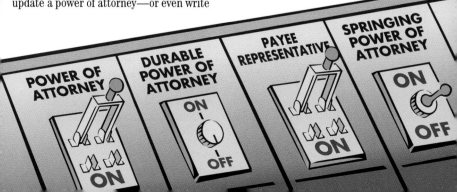

Estate Taxes

The next few years will see radical changes in estate taxes.

The advantages of a large estate—a comfortable life for yourself and gifts or inherited property for your beneficiaries—can be severely trimmed by taxes imposed on the transfer of your estate's assets. For 2004, the rate ranges from 32% to 48% for **federal estate taxes**, plus whatever additional **inheritance taxes** individual states may impose. The top federal rate is slated to drop 1% a year, to 45% in 2007, and be eliminated in 2010—at least for a year.

Estates valued at less than the exempt amount limit
PAY NO ESTATE TAX

Estates valued over the limit, left to anyone but spouse
PAY ESTATE TAX

Estates of any size, left to spouse only
PAY NO ESTATE TAX

50%* ESTATE TAX

HOW TO FIGURE ESTATE TAX

First, determine the value of the gross estate

Then, subtract the estate's expenses and reductions to find the
TAXABLE ESTATE

Next, figure the tax amount due on the value of the taxable estate

Finally, subtract the credits that apply to find the
NET ESTATE TAXES

*At 2002 rates. The rate will drop 1% a year through 2007.

WHO PAYS ESTATE TAXES?
Fewer estates than you might expect are vulnerable to taxes. Of those people who died in 2000, only 2% had estates large enough to owe tax. And the percentage of taxable estates is likely to shrink further as the size of an estate that's exempt from federal tax increases through 2009. In 2010 estate taxes will be repealed, but unless Congress takes further action, they'll be reinstated in 2011, with a tax-exempt cap of $1 million.

Year	Exemption	Highest Tax Rates
2004	$1.5 million	48%
2005	$1.5 million	47%
2006	$2 million	46%
2007	$2 million	45%
2008	$2 million	45%
2009	$3.5 million	45%
2010	REPEALED	
2011	$1 million*	55%*

*Barring further Congressional action

In 2001 rules governing taxable gifts also changed. In the past, the uniform tax credit, which determined the tax-free amount, applied to both gifts and estate value. Since 2002, the amount you can give away tax free during your lifetime is capped at $1 million. The tax rate on amounts over $1 million will be the same as the estate tax rates through 2009, but will drop to 35% in 2010.

SAVING TAXES

Although the size of the estate you can leave tax free is increasing, chances are the value of what you own has increased too. Not only should you keep careful track of what your estate is worth, but you should have an **estate plan** in place to avoid, or at least minimize, death taxes.

It's smart to create your plan with your financial and legal advisers, since the rules and regulations are complex. But the more you know about what you want to achieve, the easier (and probably cheaper) it will be to move ahead.

The plan you create should let you take advantage of several of these money-saving options:

- If you're married, you can use the **marital deduction** to leave everything in your estate to your spouse free of tax as long as your spouse is a U.S. citizen

- You can reduce the size of your estate by making annual **tax-exempt gifts**

- If you're married and your spouse agrees, you can each make an annual gift, effectively doubling the amount, even if only one of you has earned the money.

- You can make annual tax-exempt **charitable gifts** equal to half your adjusted gross income in most cases

- You can set up a **testamentary trust** in your will so that both you and your spouse can take advantage of your unified tax credit—even if your spouse's entire estate was originally yours

PAYING ESTATE TAXES

If estate taxes are due, the estate itself must pay them within nine months of your death, in most cases. It's your job, though, to anticipate the tax bill and plan so that there's enough money to pay it. If the estate doesn't pay when the tax is due, your heirs may be liable for the taxes themselves. That might mean having to sell assets at a loss, or tapping their own savings to meet the obligation, which is

RESIDENCE AND DOMICILE

Federal estate taxes are figured at the same rate no matter where you live in the U.S. But where you hang your hat can make a big difference when it comes to state taxes. For starters, real estate and tangible personal property are taxable in the state where they're physically located whether you are a resident of that state or not. Intangible personal property — stocks, for example — are taxable in the state of your legal residence, or domicile. There can only be one of those, no matter how many residences you have.

HIGH-TAX STATE

LOW-TAX STATE

If there's a question about your domicile, documents showing where you voted, maintained bank accounts, registered your car, or the residence you declared in your will can be used to prove which place you considered home. One thing you should check while you're able to is the consequences of owning property in different states. You might decide to make some changes to save taxes, or legal fees, or both.

probably not what you intended in making them your beneficiaries.

To be sure there's money available in your estate to pay the taxes, you can set up an **insurance trust** or leave instructions for **liquidating**, or turning into cash, specific assets, or selling your share of a business. The best method of coming up with the cash depends on your own financial situation. But don't assume that decisions that seem obvious to you will be just as clear to someone else. Spell out what you think should happen in a letter of instruction to your executor or your heirs.

TAKING DIFFERENT BITES

Estate taxes are taxes on the value of the property in your estate, and they're usually paid by the estate. There's a federal estate tax and, in some states, a state estate tax.

Inheritance taxes are state taxes your heirs pay for the value of the property they receive from your estate. You can specify in your will that your estate should pay whatever inheritance taxes are due to save your heirs from having to sell the property they inherit in order to be able to pay the tax.

A SEPARATE IDENTITY

Because an estate has an identity separate from the person whose property it was and from that of the executor, it needs its own federal ID number and its own bank account. You can apply for the number from the IRS using Form SS-4.

Wills

Where there's a will, there's usually a way to protect your estate.

A will is a legal document that transfers your property after you die, and names the people who will settle your estate, care for your children who are minors, and administer any trusts the will establishes. With rare exceptions, a will has to be a formal, written document that meets the legal requirements of the state where it's **executed**, or prepared. In some circumstances, a hand-written will, known as a **holograph**, passes muster. In very rare cases—usually a deathbed situation—an oral will, known as a **nuncupative** will, may be considered valid.

But why take a chance? Making a will is one situation where doing the right thing is easy and relatively inexpensive.

WHAT'S THE WORRY?

If you die **intestate**, that is without a will, you'll have lost control over what happens to your property. And your estate will probably end up paying a lot more to settle your affairs—meaning that less will be available for your heirs. Any estate, large or small, can be settled faster if you've made a will naming the people, charities, or other institutions you want to inherit your property.

If you're married and die intestate, your property will go to your spouse and any children you have. Each state has a specific formula for dividing the estate, some giving a greater percentage to the spouse and others favoring the children. If you've been married more than once, or have children from different marriages, the rules for dividing your property could produce results you wouldn't be happy about.

If you're not married, your relatives— the ones the court decides on—inherit. Chances are, what you intended to leave to friends or to charitable, religious, or

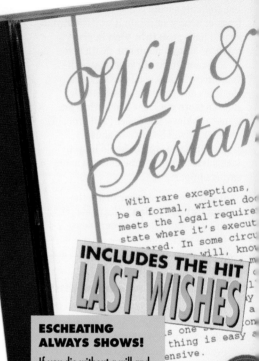

ESCHEATING ALWAYS SHOWS!

If you die without a will and have no relatives, your estate is **escheated,** or turned over, to the state where you live. That's probably how your friends will feel. About half of all Americans die intestate, including many who leave a large estate and minor children. Another 9% of existing wills are invalid for one reason or another.

educational institutions will go instead to a distant relative, perhaps one you weren't very fond of. The bottom line is that if you're unmarried, childless, and without property, you can justify waiting to make a will. Otherwise, you can't.

THE PROBATE QUESTION

Any property that is transferred by will is subject to **probate**, the legal process of proving, or verifying, your will through the courts. Because the process can be slow, costly, and sometimes perverse, probate has a bad reputation.

However, you can't avoid probate even if you don't make a will. The only thing you accomplish is to give the probate court— sometimes called surrogate's court or orphan's court—more authority over your affairs, since the court will appoint an administrator to handle your estate.

A clear, unambiguous will has the best chance of surviving the probate process without hassle or extra expense. And the more property you can transfer directly to your beneficiaries, the more you reduce potential problems.

In recent years, some people have opted for a **living trust** to transfer the bulk of their property outside the probate process. But you still need a will to leave property that isn't covered by the trust and to name an executor for your estate and a guardian for any minor children.

JOINTLY OWNED

You can't leave jointly owned property to someone other than your joint owner. If you have a joint bank account with one of your children and own your house jointly with another, that property is theirs when you die—whether or not the properties are of equal value. If your will states that your children should share your estate equally, but all your property is jointly held, your wishes can't be carried out. In fact, if one child generously equalizes her share of, say a $300,000 inheritance with her sibling, she'll be making a taxable gift of $150,000.

> **"To my children I leave...""**

> **"I name as my executor...""**

> **"To my loving husband I leave...""**

ANYTHING DOESN'T GO

You can divide your estate pretty much as you wish, though there are some things you can't do if you want your will to survive a court challenge.

WHAT YOU CAN DO

✔ You can limit the inheritance to one or more of your children, or in most states leave them nothing at all. But it's better to say so directly in the will. If you don't mention them, they might claim you simply forgot, or the laws in your state might say that children who aren't named in the will are entitled to a share of the estate, just as if you'd died intestate.

✔ You can specify whether your heirs' heirs inherit their share if the people you name die before you do.

✔ In some states, you can include an **in terrorem** clause that provides that anyone who contests your will loses whatever legacy you had provided for them. However, the court could rule there was a legitimate reason for challenging the will.

✔ You can add a legally executed **codicil**, or amendment, to your will to add, remove, or change beneficiaries or bequests.

WHAT YOU CAN'T DO

✘ No state lets you disinherit your spouse, as long as you're legally married. Most require you to leave a certain percentage of the total estate. In fact, a surviving spouse has the right to **elect against a will**. This means rejecting the terms and bequests of the will and taking instead the minimum percentage that state law sets as the spouse's share of the estate if there were no will.

✘ Louisiana won't let you disinherit your children. Several other states make it hard.

✘ You can't impose conditions on your heirs that are either illegal or against public policy. For example, if you tie an heir's right to an inheritance to a restriction on getting married or membership in a certain organization, your will might be successfully challenged.

✘ You can't write in changes or cross things out of the will after it has been signed and witnessed.

Cooking Up a Will

You can follow a number of different recipes to produce a valid will.

While wills are formal, ultimately public, documents, they're also very personal. What they're doing, after all, is detailing the size and distribution of your estate.

YOU CAN MAKE A WILL THREE WAYS

Use a standard, fill-in-the blanks will form

Use a step-by-step legal guide or computer program to draft your own

Ask your lawyer to draft a will for you

The advantages of a fill-in-the-blanks will are easy availability—you can get them in stationery stores—and economy. The major disadvantage is that they're inflexible and cover only the most generic situations, like leaving everything to your spouse. Is a fill-in-the-blanks will better than no will at all? Probably. But there's no substitute for sound legal advice.

WHAT'S BEST FOR YOU

Most experts agree that using a lawyer who specializes in wills and estates is smart, and probably essential if your estate is at all complex, involves real estate, or includes any bequests that might be challenged in court. One disadvantage may be the price tag, since a complicated will may cost a thousand dollars or more to prepare.

If you use a guidebook or computer program to write your own will, you can spend less for a perfectly legal document. It may be smart, though, to have a lawyer review your work so that your estate doesn't end up paying in court fees or estate taxes everything that you saved by writing it yourself—and more.

MAKING IT OFFICIAL

The steps to making your will official are clearly spelled out in the law. Your **execution**, or signature, has to be **attested to**, or witnessed, by two or three people who must sign the will in your presence. The witnesses don't have to read the will itself, or know what's in it, but you must tell them it's your will you're asking them to witness.

In some states a witness may not inherit anything that's included in the will, and in others people mentioned in the will may not serve as a witness. Sometimes the witnesses must appear in court when a will is filed for probate, but in many states witnesses can instead sign a document stating, or affirming, their participation at the time of the will's execution.

You should sign only one copy of your will and file it with your attorney, at home, or in some other safe place that is easy to get at. Safe deposit boxes are not a good idea, since they are frequently sealed when the owner dies, making their contents inaccessible.

If your will can't be found, the court will presume it's been revoked. On the other hand, multiple signed copies of the will can cause delays, since, in most cases, all of them must be accounted for before the will can be probated. Unsigned copies, or photocopies, on the other hand, are fine and can be useful for reference.

last wil ənd tes′ tə mənt

The sometimes elaborate and seemingly repetitive language of wills is, in part, a continuing struggle to avoid ambiguity. More often than not, legal battles over wills have been the direct result of imprecise or unclear language. The solution, over the years, has been to go on adding words to cover all the possible circumstances. That's why you use your "last **will and testament** to **give, devise, and bequeath** all the **rest, residue, and remainder** of your estate," using at least twice as many words as seem necessary to do the job.

WILL POWER

You can change your will as often as you want. There's no last word until you die, which means you can change every detail from one year to the next, and back again, as long as you're willing to foot the bill. When you make a new will, though, you should say specifically that you are revoking any prior will. If you have the old one, or copies of it, you should destroy them. That way, there will be no question about your intentions.

If you're making only minor changes, however, you can add a **codicil** to your will. Like the will itself, a codicil is a legal document that details your wishes. It must meet specific standards in order to be valid, including the requirement for witnesses.

DIVIDING YOUR ASSETS

When you divide your property among your beneficiaries, it's important to structure your will so that your wishes can be respected.

For example, suppose you leave stock to your son, but the stock has been sold? Or you leave one daughter $75,000 and everything else to another—and $75,000 is all that's left after your bills are paid?

To avoid the most common problems, experts suggest you leave all major bequests as a **percentage** of your total estate, instead of a dollar amount. You can also name contingent beneficiaries, if your first choices die before you do, can't be found, or don't want your money.

SIMULTANEOUS DEATH

Many married people leave their entire estates to their surviving spouse, and to other beneficiaries if the spouse has died first. What that doesn't resolve, however, is what happens if the couple dies at the same time, or within a very short period of each other. To cover that possibility, you can include a **simultaneous death clause** in your will to pass your property directly to your surviving heirs.

You can also require that any beneficiary survive you by a certain length of time—often 45 days—in order to inherit. This provision saves double taxes and court costs, and lets you decide who is next in line for your property.

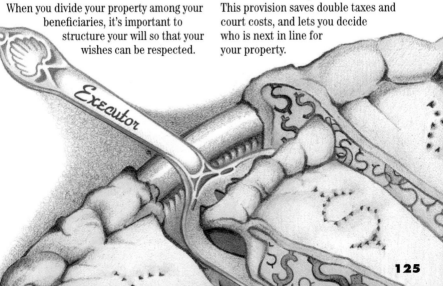

Executor

Who's in a Will?

You're the star of your will, but there's a big supporting cast.

Your will contains a list of names, starting with your own. The other people and organizations you mention either receive property when you die or have specific jobs to do. While almost anyone would be delighted to be on the receiving list, you ought to be sure that the people you're asking to carry out your wishes are willing and able to play their parts.

An **EXECUTOR**, also called a **personal representative**, to oversee settling the estate and to carry out your wishes

A **GUARDIAN**, if you have minor children

CHOOSING AN EXECUTOR

While beneficiaries don't need any special skills to qualify for inclusion in your will, executors do. The job of collecting your assets, paying your bills, and resolving legal and tax issues can be complicated and time-consuming. That means you should get the consent of the person you want to fill the executor's role. You should also name an alternative executor, should your first choice be unable or unwilling to do the job when the time comes. Otherwise the choice will be left to the probate court.

A spouse, child, or close friend is frequently named executor, and can handle the task if he or she is comfortable managing legal and financial issues. It's an added advantage if he or she can work with a family lawyer. With complex estates, however, or wills which might provoke controversy, it's often best to name an executor with professional skills. One solution may be to name joint executors, a professional and a family member or friend.

CONFLICTS OF INTEREST

If you want your will to resolve—not create—controversy over your estate, you should consider potential conflicts of interest in naming your executor.

Problems arise most often when the executor's responsibility to act in the best interests of the beneficiaries competes with his or her own best interest. For example, if your executor was your business partner and your will specified that the business should buy out your share, how would the executor set the price?

Would the goal be to add the most value to your estate or pay the least the business could get away with?

Similarly, you might create bad feelings, or even spark a contest to your will, by naming one of your children both executor and primary beneficiary of your estate. Though the conversation could be a painful one, many experts advise explaining the contents of your will to your family while you are able. That step could prevent conflict after you die.

PICKING A GUARDIAN

Children who are minors—those under 18 under the laws of most states and under 21 in the rest—need guardians if their parents die. A guardian has custody of the children and makes the decisions of daily life: Where the children live, go to school, receive medical care, and spend their vacations, are just a few of the issues. If you and your spouse each name a guardian—hopefully someone you agree on—in your will, your children should be provided for should something happen to both of you.

The primary factor for most people is naming a guardian who will raise your children as you would yourself. You choice might be

ᴅ Testament

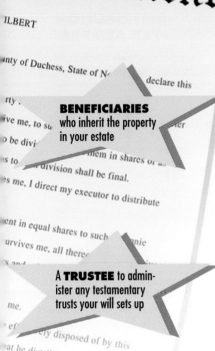

ILBERT

nty of Duchess, State of N⟨⟩ declare this

rty .

ive me, to su⟨⟩ ⟨⟩er

o be divi⟨⟩

s to ⟨⟩em in shares or ⟨⟩

⟨⟩division shall be final.

s me, I direct my executor to distribute

⟨⟩nt in equal shares to such ⟨⟩nie

urvives me, all theree⟨⟩

⟨⟩ and

me.

⟨⟩ef ⟨⟩ly disposed of by this

⟨⟩at he distribute the ⟨⟩⟨⟩

BENEFICIARIES who inherit the property in your estate

A **TRUSTEE** to administer any testamentary trusts your will sets up

a relative or a friend of yours, or even an older sibling of the children's, who will provide a good home. Someone they are already comfortable with is probably a good choice, though experts often advise against naming a grandparent because of the age factor.

Since raising children costs money, you should consider a potential guardian's financial situation as well as his or her personality before making a decision. Of course, if you leave a large estate or a lot of life insurance, the issue might be how well the guardian would manage the money. While you can name a different person to hold the purse strings—as **guardian of the property** or trustee of a trust created by your will—such an arrangement can cause complications unless the two are able to work comfortably together.

YOUR WILL ISN'T THE LAW

In some cases the probate court may overrule your choice of guardian and name another person. Relatives can also contest your will to have the guardian you name replaced by someone else, often themselves. While there's no way to prevent either situation, the more logical your choice and the more direct you are with relatives who might potentially object, the greater the chance that your wishes will prevail.

The most difficult situations are often those that involve divorced parents, or parents who disagree about who should be named. The one thing you can be sure of in such cases is that the legal battle will be long, expensive, and probably damaging to the children.

NO BONDS ATTACHED

You can specify in your will that your executor and the guardian of your minor children serve **without bond**.

Bonding is a form of insurance against fraud, designed to protect the estate against a dishonest executor. Your estate pays the bond premiums, which can be expensive, and the insurance company can slow down the process by requiring every property transfer or financial transaction to be countersigned. One thought: If you're uncertain enough about your appointee's honesty to require a bond, you'd probably be better off choosing someone else.

If you die intestate, you don't have the option of expressing your position on bonding, and it will be required.

SPOUSAL PROTECTION

Financial protection for a surviving spouse is built into state laws, usually by insuring his or her right to some part of your estate — both in cases where you leave no will and where your will is at odds with the law. Though currently your surviving spouse has a right to a share — usually a third to a half of all the assets in your estate — making sure a widow or widower isn't left out in the cold is not a new idea. In the past, a surviving widow had **dower** rights and a surviving widower had **curtesy** rights, providing life interest, or the right to use and collect income from any real estate owned by his or her spouse during the marriage.

Beneficiaries

You have a free hand in naming beneficiaries, but you'll have to leave enough to go around.

Except for the requirement of providing for your spouse, if you have one, there are no rules about who your beneficiaries, or **heirs**, are. You can leave your property to family and friends, to organizations and institutions, even to your pets. By the same token, you can leave potential heirs little or nothing.

The only legacies that are turned down with any regularity are those in which property such as a house or a collection of something is given to a charitable organization without providing money for the property's upkeep. It's hard to imagine a Picasso would be rejected anywhere, but if you're making bequests that will end up costing the beneficiary money, you ought to get approval first.

NAMING YOUR BENEFICIARIES

In naming your beneficiaries, you should be as specific as possible, especially in cases where identities might be confused. Presumably you have only one cousin named John. But if you leave him the bulk of your estate, you run fewer risks by identifying him more precisely. The same is true for colleges and universities, and for other institutions or organizations that may have similar names and may make a claim for your bequest by arguing that they have every reason to expect you to be generous. Conflicts not only create bad feelings. Any disputes that must be resolved in the courts cost money and time.

DISTRIBUTION PER STIRPES

If one child dies before you, that child's children split the share their parent would have received.

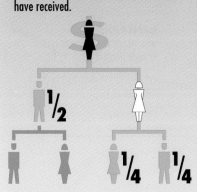

For example, if you left your entire estate equally to your two children, each of whom had two children, but one of your children died before you did, specifying the bequest as per stirpes or per capita would make a big difference to your surviving child. Under a per

KEY

🚶 You		🧍 Recipients	
🧍 Deceased		🧍 Non-Recipients	

OUTLIVING YOUR HEIRS

If you live a long life, you have to consider the possibility that the beneficiaries you name in your will may no longer be around when you die. Do you want the money you've set aside for an old friend to go to her husband if she dies before you do? If not, you can specify that your bequest is valid only if your friend survives you. If she doesn't, the money goes back into the general estate.

MULTIPLE FAMILIES

If you've been married more than once and have children from different marriages, it's important to spell out your wishes in your will. For example, if both partners in a current marriage have children of their own, they may want to leave the bulk of their own estates ultimately to their own children. If that's not clear in each partner's will, however, there could be some legitimately unhappy children.

DISTRIBUTION PER CAPITA

If one child dies before you, each surviving issue gets an equal share.

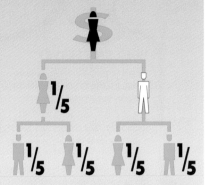

stirpes bequest, the living child would get half your estate and the two grandchildren whose parent had died would split the other half. Under a per capita bequest, however, the five (one child and four grandchildren) would get equal bequests of one fifth of your estate.

However, if you don't specify that your issue must survive you to get their share, then the heirs of your deceased children or grandchildren who may be of no relation to you — your deceased grandson's wife, for example — could claim a portion of your estate.

If the beneficiaries are your descendants, generally your children and grandchildren, known in the law as your **issue**, there is specific language you can use to designate the way your bequests will be made. If you leave an inheritance to your issue surviving you **per stirpes**, then your children's children divide the share their parent would have received. If you leave the inheritance **per capita**, then each surviving issue gets an equal share.

KEEPING UP-TO-DATE

It's important to check your will on a regular schedule—every few years, for example—to be sure it still contains the provisions you want. If there's a major change in your financial circumstances or your family structure, you should revise your will immediately. A new spouse or a new child, for example, must be taken into account. Otherwise, some sections of the outdated document, and maybe the whole thing, can be thrown out and the estate settled as if you had died intestate.

SPECIAL SITUATIONS

If you're not married, but want to leave your estate to a long-time companion, it's especially important that you have a will that makes your bequest clear. Inheritance laws don't recognize common-law marriages or any non-marital relationships, however permanent they may be to you. That's true even in states where you can register as domestic partners or qualify for benefits like health insurance coverage for your partner.

You can simplify the situation by avoiding the probate process, either by owning property jointly, or by naming your partner as beneficiary on retirement plans and insurance policies. Those assets become your partner's directly. And, you can consider creating a trust naming your partner as beneficiary. Trusts are more difficult to contest than wills, something that may be important if your family is not happy about your domestic situation.

IT'S ALL OVER

A divorce decree revokes your will, so you'll want to draw up a new will immediately, especially if there are custody issues or if you plan to remarry.

Acting as Executor

People often get a double look at this role—
acting the part and choosing the actor.

Since every will needs an executor, you may end up serving in that role as well as choosing someone to play it for you. Most people name a family member or close friend as executor or co-executor with a lawyer or other professional, even when the estate is fairly complex.

Cost is one factor: It is usually cheaper to pay a lawyer an hourly rate to handle legal issues than to act as sole executor. The personal touch is another. It's often easier for beneficiaries to relate to someone they know—though it may not always be easier on the executor if the will has unpopular or unexpected provisions to administer.

TESTATOR NAMES AN EXECUTOR

WHO CAN SERVE?

Almost anyone can serve as an executor, as long as you're no longer a minor. Some states require that you be a U.S. citizen. In addition, some states also require that you be a state resident to serve as executor unless you're a close relative. But, in others, like New York, noncitizens can serve, and even nonresident noncitizens, if they serve as co-executor with a resident. In a curious pairing of conditions, though, you're disqualified from serving as an executor if you've ever been convicted of a serious crime or if you're a judge. In any case, an executor must be confirmed by the probate court.

PROVIDING INFORMATION

A will does not ordinarily provide lists of bank and brokerage accounts, the location of your safe deposit box and its key, the details of your life insurance policies and pension plans, an inventory of valuable property, or business deals and outstanding debts. But you should provide them for your executor in a letter of instruction.

It's often true, too, that the knowledge you've accumulated—about how to liquidate a stamp collection or whether to pay off a mortgage, for example—may be as important to your heirs as the material goods you leave them. While it may seem morbid to write down that kind of information, it's a wise move.

ONLY IN THE MOVIES

You probably have a pretty clear picture of what happens when a will is read. You all gather around the lawyer, everyone listening eagerly for his or her name — and the good (or bad) news. Except it only happens that way in the movies. You're much more apt to get a letter in the mail if you're named as a beneficiary in a will.

PAYING FOR THE JOB

Executors are entitled to a fee for doing the job—usually between 2% and 5% of the value of the estate—that is paid out of the estate's assets. Some people accept the payment, and others don't. The decision is theirs, and is often based on the nature of their relationship with you and the complexity of the job. Professional executors almost always take the fee, so one way to save money is to appoint a family member who probably won't take a fee and have that person hire a lawyer to handle the more complex questions.

One case in which a family member who is also a beneficiary might take a fee for serving as executor is when estate taxes are due. The tax on the executor's added income would probably be less than the estate tax, and since the fees also reduce the estate, that might save some tax as well.

EXECUTOR

As executor you have legal and financial responsibilities that begin as soon as the **testator** — the maker of the will — dies. They involve you directly with the probate court. The process can take a few weeks, but can run a year or longer. At each step, you have to report your progress to the court. Specifically, you must:

- Present the will to the appropriate court to be probated
- Notify the people named as beneficiaries in the will
- Notify Social Security, pension administrators, insurance companies, and financial institutions
- Claim benefits payable to the estate
- Take control of the financial assets of the estate, evaluate and manage them, and collect outstanding debts
- Compute the value of the estate
- Arrange for appraisal of property not transferred by the will before it's sold or distributed at your discretion
- Pay outstanding bills, income taxes, inheritance taxes and possibly estate taxes
- Distribute willed property to heirs

EXECUTOR SETTLES THE ESTATE

THE FINAL TAX BILL

As executor of an estate, one of your jobs is to be sure that all taxes are paid — a potentially mind-numbing responsibility. Here's what's due:

$ **Potential federal estate and gift taxes**

$ **State estate or inheritance taxes, which may be owed by the estate or by individual heirs**

$ **State gift taxes (in seven states)**

$ **Generation-skipping taxes, on transfers of more than $1.5 million in 2004 and 2005, increasing to $2 million in 2006, that name grand-children or great-grandchildren as primary beneficiaries**

$ **Income taxes on the earnings of the estate's assets**

GET IN LINE

The law establishes the order in which an estate's assets are paid. Court fees, funeral expenses, and other costs of administering the estate—including executor's fees—come first, followed by taxes, medical expenses, debts, and rent or wages owed by the person who made the will. Then the other claims—including the legacies—are paid, from the most specific to the most general, or **residuary**, legacies. In general, bequests to spouses take precedence over bequests to other people.

A Matter of Trust

Once you create a trust, it takes on a life of its own.

Like a will, a **trust** is a written document that transfers property. But while a will is a statement of what you want to happen to your possessions after you die, a trust is a multipurpose tool that you can establish at any time to:

- **Manage your property**
- **Distribute assets to your beneficiaries**
- **Avoid probate**
- **Save on taxes**

Since no single trust can accomplish everything you may want to achieve, you can establish different trusts to serve different functions or benefit different people or organizations. It's also true that restrictions on the trusts vary. To reduce your taxes, for example, you have to put your property into a permanent and unchangeable trust. But trusts you established solely to manage your assets can be changed as your circumstances change.

MONEY MATTERS

Creating a trust isn't cheap. There's a legal fee—sometimes substantial—for establishing it, and a fee when you transfer ownership of the property to the trustee. The trustee is also entitled to a fee for following your wishes, filing tax returns, and overseeing the investments. Most experts agree that trusts have limited value if you're talking about property worth less than $50,000 to $75,000. Some bank trust departments, for example, set a minimum figure—usually in that range—before they'll talk to you about a trust.

HOW TRUSTS WORK

The Donor
- **Sets up the trust**
- **Names the beneficiaries**
- **Names the trustees**
- **Transfers property to the trust**

The Beneficiaries
- **Receive the benefits of the trust, according to its terms**

THREE TYPES OF TRUSTS

Though there are many different types of trusts, each designed to achieve a certain goal, all trusts are created in one of three ways.

Testamentary	Living, or inter vivos	Pour-over
A testamentary trust is created by your will, funded by your estate, and administered by a trustee named in your will. Its primary goals are saving estate taxes and appointing someone to manage the assets included in the trust.	A living, or inter vivos, trust is set up while you're alive. You can serve as the trustee yourself — though you usually name someone to succeed you when you die or if you're unable to serve. Its primary goals are asset management and transferring property outside the probate process. There may or may not be tax advantages.	A pour-over trust is created while you are alive, but funded after you die. Its primary purpose is to receive one-time payouts like life insurance or pension benefits or the residue of your estate — that is, any property you haven't transferred specifically to someone by gift, trust, or will. There may or may not be tax advantages.

TRUST ALTERNATIVES

If you want some of the advantages but not the expense of a trust, you can put your bank and brokerage accounts, as well as U.S. savings bonds, **in trust for** a beneficiary. At your death, the money goes directly to your designee, outside the probate process. It's similar to naming beneficiaries of insurance policies and employee benefit plans.

One limitation, of course, is that you can't control what your beneficiary does with the money the way you can with a trust agreement. And, though you avoid probate, the amount in these trusts is part of your estate and may be subject to estate and inheritance tax.

The Trust

- Earns income
- Pays taxes
- Distributes benefits

The Trustees

- Control the property in the trust
- Manage the trust's investments
- Oversee payments

A FIDUCIARY RELATIONSHIP

If you have fiduciary responsibility, your part of the bargain is to act in the best interests of the beneficiary or beneficiaries. In a trust, it's the trustee who is the fiduciary, acting on behalf of the beneficiary.

BENEFITS OF CREATING TRUSTS

- Taking advantage of the federal tax credits to transfer assets tax free
- Providing income to one person during his or her lifetime and, eventually, what is left to others
- Protecting assets rather than leaving them outright to heirs
- Using professional investment management
- Transferring assets outside the probate process

CREATING A TRUST

As the person creating a trust—known as a **settlor**, **donor** or **grantor**—you decide the terms of the trust, name the beneficiaries, decide which property will be included, and choose the trustee, or trustees, who will control it. You can also specify how the trust's assets will be paid to your beneficiaries, and how long the trust will last.

You specify what happens to the property you transfer to a trust by establishing the ground rules for how the assets will end up in your beneficiaries' hands. For example, you can set up a trust so that all the property goes directly to one person when you die. Or the terms of the trust might say that assets should be used for major investments like houses or business opportunities, or to pay for college tuitions.

All that information is contained in the trust document, which should be drawn up by a lawyer. You don't want to run the risk of writing your own. Since the main purpose in creating a trust in the first place is to accomplish a specific goal, it should be structured to satisfy federal and state requirements, especially through 2011, as estate tax rates and rules go through a decade of change.

Revocable Living Trusts

What's alive, in a living trust, is the person who creates it.

When you create a living trust, you must decide if it is **revocable** or **irrevocable**. If the trust is revocable, you can modify it as you wish: You can change the beneficiaries, replace the trustee, or end the trust altogether. If the trust is irrevocable, you can make no changes of any kind.

With either type of living trust you can transfer property to your beneficiaries outside the probate process, a plus for estate planning. But otherwise the two types of trusts are quite different. You choose the one that best accomplishes what you want the trust to do.

A REVOCABLE CHOICE

With a revocable trust, you can transfer as much property as you want to the trust—everything you own, for example—without owing any gift tax. That's because the property remains in your estate. When you die, the property in the trust can go directly to your beneficiary, or beneficiaries, if that's the way you set the trust up. Or, if you prefer, the trustee can continue to manage and distribute the property in the way you specify in the trust agreement.

Avoiding probate is especially valuable when you are leaving property to minors, or when you own real estate in more than one state. In those cases, going through probate can add time and expense. When property is left to minors, for example, the probate court can require continuing monitoring of the assets. And for each state where you have property, you add another probate court for your executor to deal with. If the property is passed by trust, none of that happens.

A living trust can also strengthen your intended beneficiary's claim to disputed property, since it is harder to contest a trust than a will. And since living trusts are not public information, as probate documents are, you can usually count on privacy in your bequests.

My latest revised alteration to the amendments of my Revocable LIVING TRUST

Alterations to my amended Revocable LIVING TRUST

My amended Revocable LIVING TRUST

BENEFITING YOURSELF

While the primary reason for setting up a trust is usually to benefit others, living trusts can provide advantages to the people who set them up.

While it's not a pleasant thought, people are sometimes unable to handle their affairs because of accident, illness, or age. If you've established a living trust, your trustee can protect you and your property from those who might take advantage of you, and at the same time manage your investments and pay your taxes on the trust's earnings.

Unlike someone with durable power of attorney, who can act for you only while you're alive, the trustee of a living trust can continue to manage the property in the trust after you die and for as long as the agreement remains in force. And you can simplify the process of transferring authority to your trustee by agreeing that your doctors—not the courts—can decide when you're no longer competent to act for yourself.

THREE'S A CROWD

The terms of a revocable trust permit its participants to play multiple roles.

	Donor	Beneficiary	Trustee
The donor and the beneficiary can be the same person.	●	●	○
The donor and the trustee can be the same person.	●	○	●
The trustee and the beneficiary can be the same person.	○	●	●
In some states, one person can't take all three parts. But in others, it's perfectly legal.	●	●	●

TRUST LIMITS

Revocable living trusts do have some limitations. Though they transfer the bulk of your property directly, they don't eliminate the need for a will to cover the balance of your estate after you die. And in some states your creditors may have longer to press their claims against trust property than against probate property.

But, most importantly, revocable trusts make no pretense of being tax shelters. They don't reduce the income tax you owe during your lifetime, or any estate or inheritance taxes that may be due after you die. The logic is that since you control the trust, it exists for your benefit and is therefore subject to tax.

ACTING AS TRUSTEE

As trustee, your primary job is to administer the trust in the best interest of the beneficiaries and in keeping with the wishes of the grantor. A specific problem arises if those two goals are in conflict, or if the best interests of one beneficiary are at odds with the best interests of another — say the person receiving the income from a trust and the person named to ultimately receive the principal.

As a trustee, your responsibilities are to:

- Manage trust assets to grow and produce income, which may require close supervision and ongoing decisions about what to buy and sell, and certainly means keeping accurate records

- Get the trust a tax ID number and insure that trust taxes are paid

- Distribute assets following the terms of the trust recognizing that the more discretion the trust provides about the payout terms, the more responsibility you have

- Oversee the final distribution of assets to the beneficiaries, if you're still serving as trustee when the trust ends

If you become trustee of a revocable trust because the person who set it up is no longer capable of making decisions, you may also, as a practical matter, be acting as guardian or conservator, handling living and health-care arrangements as well as finances.

A LONG HISTORY

From their beginnings in England in the 12th century, property trusts have been used to protect ownership rights — including some the courts didn't recognize. For example, when a married woman couldn't own property in her own name, she could benefit from a trust established by her family.

Irrevocable Living Trusts

Irrevocable trusts are written in stone—or its modern equivalent.

Once property is put into an irrevocable trust, it's there for good. The same is true of beneficiaries. You can't add one, or take one away. And the only way to change a trustee is for that person to agree to resign or to die. So why would anyone agree to such an inflexible arrangement? The answer, in short, is tax savings.

Irrevocable trusts can provide significant tax savings because the property you transfer to the trust is no longer yours. The trust itself—not you—pays income taxes on what the assets earn. When you die, the trust property is not part of your estate and is not subject to death taxes. What's more, through the terms of the trust, you can exert continuing control over the way that your property is distributed to your heirs.

GIVING UP CONTROL

To reduce your estate for tax purposes, though, the assets you give away or put in trust must belong permanently and unconditionally to the recipient. From the government's point of view, you no longer control the property if someone else has the legal right to decide what to do with it, or if it's part of a trust that you can't change your mind about.

TAXING ISSUES

One of the disadvantages of transferring property to an irrevocable trust is that most of a trust's earnings are taxed at the highest individual income tax rate—currently 35%.

In some cases, that could even mean that trust income is being taxed at a higher rate than you're paying as an individual—an unkind irony.

One way a trust can reduce its income tax is by distributing the earnings to the beneficiaries, so the money is spread around to be taxed at lower rates. But that solution may be at odds with your other goals for the trust, such as asset growth to provide greater income in the future, or limiting the current disposable income of your beneficiaries.

The alternative is to have the beneficiaries pay tax on the distributions but agree to allow the assets to remain in the trust, where they can continue to compound.

THOU SHALT NOT

Control the Property

Change the Beneficiary

Alter the Trustees

and verily

THOU SHALT SAVE ON TAXES

TRUST

The Squeeze on Trusts

The tax brackets for trust income are much narrower than the brackets for individual income. For example, trust assets valued at $100,000 providing an 8% annual return would fall into the highest marginal tax bracket.

TAX RATE*	APPLIES TO INCOME
15%	Up to $1,950
25%	Between $1,950 and $4,600
28%	Between $4,600 and $7,000
33%	Between $7,000 and $9,550
35%	Over $9,550

allow distributions "for the

TRUSTS AND TAXES

When you set up a trust and transfer assets to it, you have to consider the tax consequences. You can give the trust up to $1 million without owing federal gift taxes. But if you transfer more than that, the tax will be due, at the same rates as estate taxes through 2009, and at the top individual tax rate in 2010.

Some states have gift taxes, too, and impose them on smaller gifts than the federal government does. So you might owe state taxes, but not federal taxes. Often the biggest benefit from setting up an irrevocable trust is that any appreciation of the trust's assets after the date of the gift doesn't increase the value of your estate.

PLANNING AHEAD

Despite the shrinking income tax savings and the potential drawback of parting with your property while you're still alive, an irrevocable living trust is an ideal way to pass property to your heirs. That's because the one change you can make to an irrevocable trust is to add assets to it. If you make annual tax-exempt gifts, you're reducing your estate while protecting the property until you think your beneficiary is wise enough to use the assets in ways you would approve. But you must be certain the trust is set up with **Crummey** power, to meet tax-exempt requirements.

One smart idea may be to put assets that you expect to increase in value, or cash to buy those assets, into a trust. For example, you can put stock valued at $11,000 into a trust called a **qualified minor's trust** you set up for your daughter. You're within the annual tax-free gift limit. And when the trust terminates and the property becomes hers outright, it will be worth whatever the current value of the stock is—presumably but not necessarily more than its original price. By using the trust, you've not only saved gift taxes on the current gift, but also on the **appreciated value** of the stock. You've also reduced income and estate taxes because the property no longer belongs to you.

A CRUMMEY CHOICE

You can add up to the annual gift exclusion in cash or other assets to an irrevocable trust every year without owing gift tax, thanks to D. Clifford Crummey, who won a court case against the IRS in 1968. The only conditions are that the beneficiary must have the right to withdraw the gift within a fixed time period and has to be notified of that right. You choose the time at which the trust will end, and the assets become the beneficiary's property. Until that date, you can act as trustee or appoint someone else to the job.

SKIP LIGHTLY

If you create a trust to benefit your grandchildren or their children, or anyone two or more generations younger than you are, it's known as a **generation-skipping trust**.

As long as the assets in the trust are $1.5 or less in 2004 and 2005 (or double if a husband and wife each create a trust) the transfer is exempt from the **generation-skipping tax (GST)**. If the assets are more, they're taxed using a complex formula based on the maximum federal estate tax rate, on top of whatever estate or gift taxes are due. The exempt amount increases gradually to $3.5 million in 2009, and the law is slated for repeal in 2010. But permanent repeal requires further Congressional action.

If you establish a trust to pay for your grandchild's—or any child's—college expenses, the annual amount counts as income to the child's parents in some states. The logic is that it's the parents' responsibility to provide for their children's education.

SPENDTHRIFT CLAUSES

If you're creating a trust because you're nervous about a beneficiary's ability to handle money, most states let you put on the brakes with a safety device known as a **spendthrift clause**. That way, borrowing against principal and any future income is limited, and the funds are protected from creditors—at least until the money is actually paid. So even if you can't control the spending speed, you can limit the refueling rate.

Testamentary Taxsavers

Creating a trust in your will lets you do good to others and well by your estate.

Like any other trust, a testamentary trust protects your assets while providing for your heirs. Unlike a living trust, where you part with your property while you're still alive, a testamentary trust is created by your will after you die. You choose the beneficiaries and set the terms that the trustee follows in paying out the assets. You can establish how long the trust will last and who gets what's left.

THE ESTATE ADVANTAGE

If your estate is valued at less than the amount you can leave tax free, or if you give away most of your property before you die, you may decide that there's no need to establish a testamentary trust.

There are several advantages to using a trust, however. One is that you can establish how the assets are to be paid out to your heirs. And if you select a trustee who is good with money, the assets should continue to grow and produce even more income.

Finally, you can structure a **bypass trust** so that someone—usually your spouse—benefits from the trust during his or her lifetime while the principal is set aside for your other beneficiaries. Your spouse or other designee gets the income from the trust, and can be given the power to withdraw up to 5% of the assets, or $5,000 a year, whichever is greater.

If this first beneficiary doesn't need the money, it can be left to grow undisturbed. And if the trust's value has doubled or tripled by the time your spouse dies, there's still no estate tax due because the value of the trust, for tax purposes, was set at the time you died.

BETTER LATE...

Your heirs can sometimes do estate planning after your death by *disclaiming*, or renouncing, your bequest. Your spouse, for example, could disclaim the right to inherit a share of your estate to take advantage of your estate tax exemption, allowing your children to inherit directly.

SAVING TAXES

A testamentary trust can limit the taxes on the estate of a married couple by allowing each partner to take advantage of the federal estate tax exemption. Trusts that are set up to take advantage of this tax-saving feature are variously known as **family, bypass, credit shelter**, or **exemption equivalent** trusts.

Remember, though, the only property that can be put into a testamentary trust is property you own outright. Some

With a Will Only

You can leave an estate worth up to the exempt amount free of federal tax to anyone you choose. If you're married, and leave your entire estate to your spouse tax free, it becomes part of his or her estate.

HUSBAND

LEAVE ESTATE TO WIFE

Your spouse can leave an estate equal to the exempt amount tax free, even if your combined estates are worth more than that.

WIFE

LEAVE COMBINED ESTATE TO HEIRS

HEIRS

ESTATE OWES TAX ON AMOUNT OVER EXEMPT AMOUNT

A SPRINKLING TRUST

If you establish a trust with a number of beneficiaries — your children or grandchildren for instance — you can give your trustee sprinkling powers. That way, if one beneficiary needs more income than the others, or if an uneven distribution would save on taxes, the trustee can sprinkle the benefits around rather than following a stricter formula.

legal experts advise, therefore, that couples with substantial accumulated wealth split some of their jointly held assets. That way, each of them is able to fund a testamentary trust to take full advantage of the tax credit. In splitting joint assets, however, it may be wiser to divide investment assets—like stocks or bonds—rather than give up joint ownership of your home.

MARITAL TRUST

Even though you can leave your entire estate to your spouse tax free, you might want to establish a **marital trust** to oversee the estate's management or the way it is distributed after your spouse's death. As long as your spouse has the right to the income from your estate for life, the marital deduction will still apply, and no estate tax will be due, no matter how large the estate.

Since the remaining value of the marital trust is added to your spouse's estate when he or she dies, that estate may have to pay taxes if it's larger than the exclusion amount. But there can be both immediate and long-term benefits if your spouse is inexperienced or uneasy about managing money, or if you're concerned about who will ultimately benefit from your estate.

One kind of marital trust gives your spouse the right to distribute the property you leave in trust as he or she chooses. In legal language, that's known as a **general power of appointment**. The chief benefit of such a trust, from your perspective, is the financial management your trustee will provide.

With a **qualified terminable interest property trust, or QTIP**, however, you choose the ultimate beneficiaries of the trust—those who will get the income or principal of the trust after your spouse's death. If you want to insure that your assets will go to your children from a previous marriage, for example, this type of trust lets you do it.

With a Testamentary Trust

HUSBAND

However, if you've created a testamentary trust funded with up to the exempt amount of your assets, that is not part of your spouse's estate. It goes to your heirs free of estate tax.

WIFE

LEAVE ASSETS IN TESTAMENTARY TRUST

LEAVE ASSETS IN TESTAMENTARY TRUST

Then, when your spouse dies, the value of the second trust goes to your heirs tax free. Since there's no way to be sure which spouse will die first, the wills of both spouses should provide for a testamentary trust.

HEIRS

HEIRS GET ASSETS IN BOTH TRUSTS FREE OF ESTATE TAX

WILL THE SUN SET?

The 2001 tax law, which gradually increases the size of the estate you can leave tax free and eliminates the estate and generation-skipping taxes entirely in 2010, has a **sunset provision**. That means that unless Congress votes to make the repeal permanent, the tax-exempt amount will revert to $1 million in 2011. Uncertainty about that decision makes effective planning an even greater challenge.

The Universe of Trusts

The outer limits of the trust universe haven't been reached yet—and they may never be.

If you've got assets to protect or give away, you can probably create a trust to do the job. And in some cases, there are extra benefits—like charitable deductions on your income tax—in the bargain. Getting it right can be tricky, though. In some cases, for example, if you die within three years of transferring assets to a trust, the property is counted in your estate anyway. That's just one example of rules and regulations that govern the universe of trusts.

IT'S BETTER TO GIVE... AND RECEIVE

If you create a living trust to give money to a charitable institution, there are some added benefits. That's because the trust not only reduces your estate and ultimately your estate taxes—but also lets you take a charitable deduction to reduce your income taxes in the year you establish the trust. Perhaps best of all, you can either get the income earned by the assets in the trust, or your heirs get the trust balance back after a specific period of time, with no capital gains tax due on the assets that are sold.

A **charitable gift annuity** is an outright gift to a charity in return for a current tax deduction and an income stream while you live, or while you and your spouse live. The amount of the deduction depends on your life expectancy and the current interest rate. The income depends on your age, whether the annuity covers one life or two, and the size of the gift. The older you are at the time of the gift, the larger your annuity will be.

A **charitable remainder trust** is designed to pay you or someone you choose current income, either for a set period of time up to 20 years, or for life. When the beneficiaries die, what's left in

the trust—the remainder—goes to the charity. If the trustee sells the appreciated or nonincome-producing assets once they are in the trust and replaces them with income-producing investments, the amount you or your beneficiary receive as income can increase as well.

The size of the charitable deduction you can take when you fund this type of charitable trust is figured using government valuation rules, and may not be the same as fair market value. You should consult your tax adviser or the IRS.

With a **charitable lead trust**, a charity gets annual income generated by the assets for a number of years specified in the trust agreement. When the trust ends your heirs get back what's left. The advantage is that the gift to your heirs is valued at a reduced gift tax cost, based on IRS tables, since your heirs won't benefit from it until sometime in the future. The discounted present value applies, no matter how much the principal appreciates during the life of the trust.

LIFE INSURANCE TRUSTS

While the whole issue of how much life insurance you need is complicated and controversial, it pays to be aware of how a large life insurance payout can affect the size of your estate—and the resulting estate taxes. While your heirs don't pay income tax on the insurance they receive when you die, if the death benefit pushes your estate over the exemption limit, estate taxes will kick in. You can usually avoid this situation by excluding the insurance from your estate.

One way to do this is to have another person own the insurance policy on your life. If you die, the insurance goes to the owner. Another solution is to have the policy owned by an insurance trust, so that the payout goes to the trust. Though there are some tricky legal issues to work out, you can pay the premiums and trustee's fees yourself with yearly gifts to the trust. You can also specify the ultimate beneficiaries of the trust, and any conditions that the trustee must follow.

A third alternative is a **second-to-die insurance policy**, which covers both spouses but pays nothing until the second one dies. The payout can then be used to pay any estate taxes that are due. However, unless you and your spouse have a combined estate worth substantially more than the amount the two of you together can leave tax free, this option may not be worth the cost of the insurance.

Each of these strategies has advantages and limitations—and yards of red tape. Consult your tax adviser before you decide to use any one of them and to determine which is best for you.

WATCH OUT FOR SCAMS

Since trusts are attractive, profitable, and often customized tools, they have also become a haven for scam artists. More and more "con-trusts" pop up every year. These trusts commonly promise a 100% tax shelter and can come under names such as Pure Trusts, Freedom Trusts, and Patriot Trusts to name only a few. But beware: Users of these trust schemes that improperly evade tax are held responsible, whether they knowingly invested in the scam or not. That means they're liable for taxes, interest, and civil penalties.

TRUST OF THE HOUR

Though you wouldn't think so, there are fads in trusts just as there are fads in other things. Over the years a number of different trusts have been widely used before being eliminated by revisions to the tax code. Often those changes have been made to correct what seemed to be unfair practices. Other types of trusts have faded from view because they didn't provide the expected benefits. The bottom line before you set up any trust is weighing the advantages—mostly financial— against the hassles and set-up costs. Sad but true, the more perfect the idea sounds, the more likely it is to have hidden or not-so-hidden drawbacks, usually involving property that goes back into your estate so that you lose the entire advantage of setting up the trust in the first place.

BLIND TRUSTS

Instead of protecting your assets for your heirs, blind trusts are designed to protect your reputation for integrity if you hold public office. When you set up a blind trust, you transfer complete control of your assets to a trustee. Equally as important, you're kept in the dark about what happens to them: You don't know what's bought or sold, or what's making money or losing money.

The point of all this? The decisions you make as an elected or appointed official aren't tainted by the suspicion that you're acting in your own financial interest.

Gifts

From a tax perspective, there's more to giving gifts than meets the eye.

If the key to minimizing estate taxes is to reduce your estate, then giving gifts will get the job done. Before you start spreading money around, though, it pays to consider the benefits and the limitations of generosity.

You can give anyone you choose a tax-free gift of cash or other property valued at up to the exempt amount each year, for as many years as you like. That's $11,000 for 2004, an amount that will be increased in $1,000 increments in future years, indexed to increases in inflation.

While such gifts aren't tax-deductible, you pay no tax when the gift is made and neither does the recipient. If your spouse joins in the gift, together you can give each person up to twice the limit each year, with each of you considered to have given half.

You can also make gifts larger than the $11,000 annual exemption without owing gift tax until your cumulative taxable lifetime gifts exceed $1 million. When you hit that mark, you owe tax at the same rate as the estate tax through 2009, and at 35% for 2010.

Even if tax is not due, you have to report gifts valued at $25,000 or more to the IRS on Form 709 that you file with your income tax return.

In addition to the big bump in your lifetime gift exclusion, the amount you can give in gifts and the size of the estate you can leave tax free are no longer linked. In effect, that means that in 2005, for example, you could make gifts worth $1 million and leave an estate valued at $1.5 million free of tax. Remember, though, that these laws could change at any time.

GIFTS TO MINORS

If you want to make gifts to children but not just give them the cash, you can set up custodial accounts using either the **Uniform Gifts to Minors Act (UGMA)** or the **Uniform Transfer to Minors Act (UTMA)**, to protect the accumulating assets. There's no charge for setting up or administering the account, and you can build it regularly without owing gift taxes as long as you add no more than the exempt amount each year. That's a combined total, though, of all gifts to the same person, including those under UGMA or UTMA.

One advantage of UTMAs is that you can include assets that don't produce regular earnings, like real estate and paintings, in addition to cash and securities, such as stocks and bonds.

THEY CAN TAKE IT WITH THEM

If you can live with the idea that the child will take control of the assets in a UGMA or UTMA account at age 18, 21, or 25 depending on state law, it's a simple way to pass along your assets. While you're not required to liquidate the account and hand over cash to the child on the date of majority, bear in mind that on that date the child has the right to the money and can demand it.

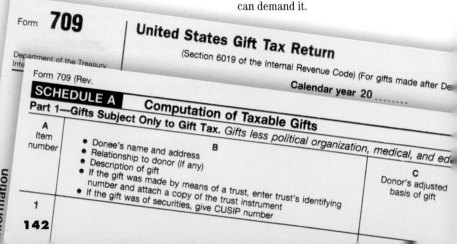

SPECIAL CONSIDERATION

There are some other things to think about with UGMAs and UTMAs that might influence the way you make your gifts:

1 First, any assets a young person has in his or her own name can reduce college financial aid. That's because a student is expected to contribute a greater percentage of savings to pay college costs than a parent is.

2 Second, if you name yourself the custodian of the account and you die while the child is still a minor, the value of the account is included in your estate—completely defeating the purpose for which it was established. You can get around this problem by naming another adult as custodian.

3 Third, since children under 14 pay tax on earnings at their parents' rate, you might consider giving growth rather than income investments to minimize the tax bite.

GIFTS TO OTHERS

The annual tax-exempt limit applies to gifts you make to people of all ages, not just minors. For gift tax purposes, the value of the gift is its value at the time it is given—not what it was when you acquired it. If the item is worth more when you give it than it's been worth in the past, you don't have to pay capital gains on the increased value. However, if the person receiving the gift sells it, she will owe capital gains based on its **cost basis**, or your original cost, which might result in a sizeable tax bill.

SPECIAL GIFTS

If you want to pay for someone's educational expenses, you can make a tax-exempt gift to the college or university equal to the cost of tuition. The understanding is that the student's bill will be considered paid. You can't pay for room and board this way, but tuition is usually the bulk of the cost in any case. The same option exists for paying hospital bills. The process is known as a **qualified transfer**, and there don't seem to be any restrictions on qualifying. Plus, these payments do not limit your right to give up to the exempt amount per year to the beneficiary of the transfer as a tax-exempt gift.

TAX-FREE GIFTS

If your spouse is a U.S. citizen, you may give him or her as much as you want, as often as you want, without owing gift taxes. But the picture changes when your spouse is the citizen of another country. Then, there's a $114,000 annual limit in 2004 on tax-exempt gifts and, without special planning involving the use of a **qualified domestic trust (QDOT)**, no **marital deduction.** That is, you can't leave your spouse your entire estate outright free of federal tax.

Tax-exempt gifts to charities, like gifts to your spouse, aren't capped, but they are limited to a percentage of your adjusted gross income. Check with your tax adviser or the IRS for the rules that apply to various kinds of gifts.

And More Gifts

It's hard-headed, not hard-hearted, to think about what your gifts will cost you and your estate.

When you're considering making a gift, you probably ought to consider the tax consequences of the way you give it. For example, if the choice is between giving property you own, or selling the property and making a cash gift, the size of the gift makes a big difference.

And if the choice is between making a gift or leaving the same property as a legacy in your will, you need to think about **cost basis**, the value assigned to the property that the recipient gets. It could make a major tax difference if he or she sells the property.

MAKING THE MOST OF A DEAL

When you make a charitable gift, you can take a tax deduction for the value of the property. In most cases, it makes the most sense to contribute appreciated assets — those that have increased in value since you bought them — because you can deduct the current value and avoid capital gains on the increase in value.

for example

Purchase shares of stocks costing	$ 10,000
Value of shares at time of gift	$ 40,000

GIVE THE STOCK Vs. **SELL THE STOCK AND GIVE THE CASH**

YOU	THE CHARITY	YOU	THE CHARITY
• Take deduction based on current value ($40,000)	• Gets benefit of full value of your donation ($40,000)	• Pay capital gains tax on profit: $30,000 x .15* = $ 4,500 TAX	• Receives only $35,000 instead of $40,000
• Owe no capital gains tax		• Take deduction on only $35,500 gift	

*Tax at 15% capital gains rate.

GIFTS TO TRUSTS

Money you put into a trust is considered a gift in some circumstances, but not others. In general, the difference hinges on whether or not the trust is revocable or irrevocable, and who the beneficiary is.

Revocable trusts don't result in gift taxes because the transfer of property is considered incomplete. That's because you can change your mind about what's in the trust and who benefits.

But if the trust is irrevocable, gift taxes apply if the beneficiary is anyone but yourself or your spouse. In fact, if you're the beneficiary of an irrevocable trust during your lifetime, the property you put into the trust is considered a gift to your surviving beneficiaries. You figure the value based on U.S. Treasury department tables that are included with the rules on gift taxes.

Give It or Leave It

If you're undecided whether to make gifts now or leave property as a legacy in your will, you can balance a variety of pluses and minuses for each option.

GIFTS

Advantages	Disadvantages
• If you spread gifts over the years you can provide generously for your beneficiaries and reduce your estate at the same time	• Once a gift is given, you don't have access to it even if you need it
• Your gift may be worth more to the beneficiary since it's not subject to estate and inheritance taxes	• You can't control how gifts are used
• You can help meet financial needs when they occur	• Your heir may end up owing capital gains tax if he or she sells the gift, but the silver lining is that capital gains taxes are lower than estate taxes

LEGACIES BY WILL

Advantages	Disadvantages
• You keep your assets as long as you need them	• Wills can be contested
• You can change your mind about items left in your will until the last minute	• Federal estate taxes may reduce the size of your legacy
• For your heir, the cost basis of the asset—the starting point for figuring capital gains—is currently the value at the date of your death. That could save taxes if the assets were sold	• Your heir may owe state inheritance taxes
	• Under current law, cost basis may be eliminated in 2010, and your heir may face large capital gains taxes

FAMILY LIMITED PARTNERSHIPS
Another approach to using gifts to pass valuable property to your children and grandchildren has been to create a **family limited partnership (FLP)**. The parents, or senior family members, serve as general partners and maintain control over the assets in the partnership, usually real estate or a family business. The junior members of the family are limited partners, with no current authority but a growing share of the partnership assets.

Each year, each general partner can give each limited partner a share in the assets as a tax free gift. And they're allowed to transfer the assets at a discount to face value. For example, the actual value of the gift might be closer to $14,000 than the $11,000 limit. The discount is legitimate if there's a valid business purpose for the partnership.

The value of the gift may be also be discountable because the shares are usually not attractive to potential buyers. An FLP may give existing partners the right of first refusal or allow them to exclude an outsider from the partnership. If you're considering such a partnership, you should consult an experienced legal adviser. Among the reasons: The IRS tends to question FLPs.

GIVER BEWARE
If the Tax Relief Act of 2001 doesn't expire in 2011, as it's currently scheduled to do, and the estate tax is permanently repealed, some major changes are in store. Chief among them is the modification of the step up in basis provision. That means the value of assets you leave in your will may be inherited at your adjusted cost basis instead of at their value at the time of your death. That could result in substantial capital gains tax for your heirs if the assets are sold.

Protecting Health and Wealth

Insurance is essential to creating a healthy financial plan.

You can work hard at staying healthy. But you need health insurance to help pay the costs of routine care and the possibility, however unwelcome, of serious illness or accident.

Without insurance, the money you've saved or invested to meet your financial goals could be eaten up by hospital and doctor bills. Even worse, uninsured healthcare costs can quickly drain a family's physical and emotional as well as financial resources, sometimes to the breaking point.

A BENEFIT, NOT A RIGHT

For many people in the workforce, health insurance is a key employee benefit. The availability of a plan, as well as the quality of coverage it provides, can be a deciding factor in taking a job.

If your employer does offer health insurance, you may be able to choose from a limited number of plans and have your **premium**, or cost of coverage, deducted from your salary. In some cases, employers cover the basic premium, and you pay only for added benefits or family coverage. In other cases, employers pick up some of the cost, and you pay the rest.

GETTING YOUR OWN COVERAGE

Remember, though, that employers aren't required to offer health insurance. If you need to find coverage on your own because your employer doesn't offer it, you work for yourself, or you don't work, cost can be a primary concern.

Since group health insurance is almost always more affordable than an individual plan, you can start your search with groups that you belong to, such as alumni, professional, or religious associations. If you can't get group insurance, then you'll have to look for an individual policy. The good news is that you can tailor your coverage to your needs. For example, you might choose a **major medical policy** that begins to cover your care only after you've laid out several thousand dollars. That means you'll be paying a much lower than average premium.

Keep in mind that when you arrange coverage on your own you'll probably have to pass a physical exam to qualify, something you don't have to do when enrolling in an employer's plan. There's always the chance you could be turned down, especially if you have a health problem, or what's known as a **pre-existing condition**.

Once you find individual insurance, you're also responsible for keeping your policy in force. If you miss a payment, you risk having the policy cancelled.

TYPES OF

There are two basic types of health care coverage, **traditional health insurance plans**, also called fee-for-service (FFS) or point-of-service (POS) plans, and **managed care plans**, such as a health maintenance organization (HMO) or a preferred provider organization (PPO).

TRADITIONAL

With a traditional plan, you choose your own doctors, pay your medical bills, and submit a claim for reimbursement. Most traditional plans have a **deductible**, or fixed dollar amount, which you must pay for healthcare costs before your insurance benefits begin. For example, with a $300 deductible, you must pay $300 in cash—called out-of-pocket costs—before the insurance company starts to pay. Once you reach your deductible, most traditional plans cover 70% to 80% of the charges they approve for the treatment you've had. Some plans approve charges that come close to what you've spent, while others set their approved rates much lower. You pay the balance.

COVERAGE

Both types of plans cover approved hospital stays and doctors' bills. Certain plans cover care provided by other health professionals, prescription drugs, mental health care, and dental care. Or you may be able to pay extra to get the added coverage.

MANAGED CARE

With a managed care plan, you pay a **copayment** or **coinsurance**—interchangeable terms for your cost—each time you receive healthcare. That could be a dollar amount—say $15 or $20—or a percentage of your bill, perhaps 20% to 40%. Those amounts are subject to change whenever the coverage is renewed.

Managed care plans also differ from traditional insurance because they work with **networks**, or affiliated groups of caregivers. To have your care covered, you usually have to see a doctor in the network. And with many plans, you have to be referred for that care by your doctor, also called your **primary care provider** or **gatekeeper**. Managed care also differs from traditional insurance in another important way—it often covers preventative care.

THE LAW'S ON YOUR SIDE

You have the legal right to be covered under a new employer's plan if you move from a job that provided you with health insurance. And **COBRA**, the Consolidated Omnibus Reconciliation Act of 1985, allows you to pay for continued coverage under your old employer's plan if you quit, are laid off, or retire. In most cases, you can extend the coverage for 18 months, or up to 29 months if you're disabled.

Your dependents are eligible for three years of COBRA coverage under the same terms as you are—at 102% of your employer's cost—when they no longer qualify for coverage under your plan. That might happen if you die, if you and your spouse are legally separated or divorced, or if your children aren't full-time students after they turn 19.

COBRA also gives you and your former dependents the option of buying a **conversion policy**. That's an individual policy with the same company that provides your group plan. You usually get fewer benefits than you would through the group plan even though you'll pay a higher premium. But if you can't get insurance on your own, or by asking for help from your state's Insurance Department, a conversion policy may be your best alternative.

COBRA COVERAGE

HEALTH SAVINGS ACCOUNTS

If your employer offers a **high deductible health plan (HDHP)** or you establish one for yourself if you're self-employed or own a small business, you are eligible to open a **health savings account (HSA)**. Contributions are tax deductible and you may withdraw your contributions plus any earnings tax free at any time to pay for qualified healthcare expenses.

With most plans, you can add up to the full amount of your plan's deductible to your account each year, and if you're between 55 and 65 you can make an annual catch-up contribution. It's $500 in 2004 and $600 in 2005. You can roll over any money you don't spend in one year to cover expenses in later years.

Medicare

One benefit of turning 65 is that you're eligible for Medicare.

Medicare, the federal government's health insurance plan for people over 65, has made an enormous difference in the healthcare of an entire generation of Americans.

If you qualify for Social Security either because you made FICA contributions while you were working or you're married to someone who did, you automatically qualify for Medicare. And even if you weren't part of the Social Security system, you may be eligible to purchase Medicare coverage for a modest annual fee.

MAKING MEDICARE CHOICES

If you're collecting Social Security benefits, you're automatically enrolled in both Parts A and B, though you have a choice of whether to keep Part B. If you enroll for Medicare before you apply for Social Security benefits, you must decide whether to sign up for Part B.

The second round of choices may be more complicated. Provided you've taken Part B coverage, you may be able to choose how you want to receive Medicare services, through **original Medicare** or what is known as **Medicare+Choice**.

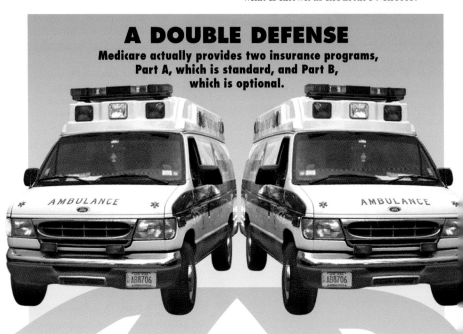

A DOUBLE DEFENSE

Medicare actually provides two insurance programs, Part A, which is standard, and Part B, which is optional.

Part A provides hospitalization insurance for everyone who qualifies for or buys Medicare, as well as limited coverage for other in-patient care, such as a nursing home stay or home healthcare.

Part B is optional insurance that covers medical services, such as doctors' bills, medical equipment, tests, and some preventative health care, such as vaccinations, colorectal and prostate cancer screening, mammograms, and Pap smears. But it doesn't cover routine check-ups, prescription drugs, or treatment outside the U.S.

TIME FRAMES

Part A coverage is measured in benefit periods. A period begins the first day you are admitted to a hospital and ends when you've been out of the hospital for 60 consecutive days. A new period begins the next time you enter a hospital. Each time a new benefit period begins, you're responsible for the deductible, but there's no limit on the number of benefit periods for which you are covered.

Part B Medicare coverage works on an annual calendar. You pay the year's premium in monthly installments, and you are responsible for the annual deductible. Once you've paid that out-of-pocket amount, Medicare covers its share of whatever claims are submitted during the year. You pay the balance of the bill.

Original Medicare—the only Medicare plan that existed between 1967 and 1997—is still the most popular choice, and the only option available in many parts of the country. It's a fee-for-service plan that resembles traditional health insurance.

Within the **Medicare+Choice** program, you may also have two alternatives, depending on what's available where you live. One option is **managed care plans**, most commonly health maintenance organizations (HMOs) that accept Medicare members. The other is **private fee-for-service (FFS)** plans that work like traditional health insurance.

Both have advantages and some potential drawbacks, including the insurer's right to decide whether or not treatment is medically necessary.

PAYING FOR MEDICARE

Medicare Part A is funded by the payroll withholding tax on the salaries of all working people and a matching amount from their employers. You don't pay anything additional for the services you receive.

You pay for Part B, by having the monthly premium deducted from your Social Security check if you get one. If not, you pay the premium directly. The cost, which is $66.60 a month for 2004 and $78.20 for 2005, has risen much faster than the rate of inflation. An otional drug benefit will be available in 2006.

AN INDIVIDUAL PLAN

Medicare covers individuals, not families. Spouses who aren't yet 65 must have their own health insurance until they're old enough to be eligible for Medicare.

HOW TO ENROLL

If you start receiving Social Security before you're 65, you'll get your Medicare enrollment card in the mail. And if you apply to begin Social Security benefits when you turn 65, you can apply for Medicare at the same time.

But if you're still working, want to postpone collecting Social Security, or don't yet qualify for your full benefit, you've got to apply for Medicare on your own. If you apply after you're initially eligible, you risk delays in coverage. More seriously, if you apply late for Part B coverage, you risk an additional 10% surcharge on your premium for each year that you were eligible but didn't enroll.

The Seven-month Window

← 3 MONTHS BEFORE	THE MONTH OF YOUR 65TH BIRTHDAY	3 MONTHS AFTER →
You can apply up to three months before your 65th birthday. If you do, your coverage begins as soon as you reach 65.	If you enroll in the month you turn 65, coverage begins on the first of the following month.	If you enroll within the next three months, there's a two-month wait. Medicare doesn't cover any of your Part B bills during that period.

If you miss that deadline...

General Enrollment

Jan 1–Mar 31

If you miss the deadline, you have to wait until the next general enrollment period—January 1 to March 31 each year—to sign up.

COVERAGE BEGINS
↓

J F M A M J J A S O N D

For example, if your 65th birthday was in April and you hadn't applied by the end of July, you couldn't enroll until the next January, and your coverage couldn't begin until the following July.

ALWAYS AN EXCEPTION

The rules are different, though, if you're still working at age 65 and have employer-provided insurance. Then you can delay applying for Part B coverage until you need it, and your premium won't be increased. You might find, however, that your employer encourages you to switch to Part B when you first become eligible. In fact, the company might even pick up the cost of the Part B premium, because it would cost less than covering you through the group policy.

Making Medicare Choices

There are several choices for covering your healthcare needs.

While having to deal with several rounds of Medicare decisions can be intimidating, there is a bright side. You're arranging for coverage that can help protect your financial as well as your physical health.

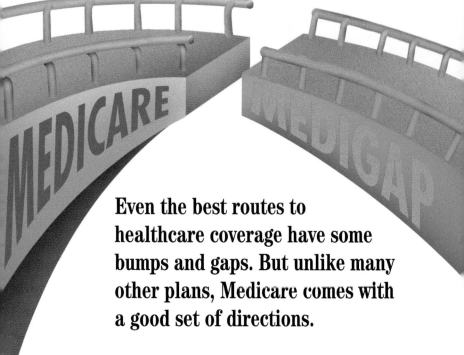

Even the best routes to healthcare coverage have some bumps and gaps. But unlike many other plans, Medicare comes with a good set of directions.

BRIDGING A GAP

If you enroll in original Medicare, you have to pay for:

- **A 20% copayment for approved medical services**
- **An increasing percentage of your bill during the first 150 days you're hospitalized and the total cost after 151 days**
- **The cost of prescription drugs**
- **All uncovered expenses**

As a way to protect your financial security, you can buy **Medigap**, an insurance plan designed to bridge these gaps in your coverage.

Medigap insurance isn't a one-size-fits-all solution. There are actually ten different plans labeled A through J available from insurance companies. Each plan offers a slightly different combination of benefits, from bare-bones to comprehensive. Plan A is the core package: It covers coinsurance for hospitalizations longer than 60 days, the 20% coinsurance for medical care, and three pints of blood. All insurers offer Plan A.

Since each state decides how many of the plans in addition to Plan A can be sold to its residents, you may not be able to choose from the full range of options. But it's easy to compare those that are available to you because all policies designated by the same letter offer the same coverage, regardless of which companies provide them. The only differences are the cost of coverage from different insurers and the efficiency with which those insurers resolve your claims.

CINDERELLA PLANS

Your employee health plans may turn into a Medigap plan after you retire, rather than continuing to provide the type of coverage you had while you were working. Or your employers may ask you to choose a Medigap plan and give you money to pay the premium.

IT'S YOUR CHOICE

If you decide to take one of the plans offered through Medicare+Choice, either managed care or private fee-for-service, you'll still be enrolled in the Medicare system and entitled to at least as much coverage as with original Medicare. But on a day-to-day basis, you'll deal directly with your plan's representatives, not Medicare's.

You'll still pay your Part B premium, which is the same for everyone, to Medicare. But if your plan's premium is higher—and it probably will be—you pay that amount directly to the plan. The added expense reflects the fact that most plans offer broader coverage than Medicare.

For example, you may be covered for prescription drugs or long hospital stays.

GETTING IN AND OUT

Most Medicare+Choice plans enroll new Medicare patients in November, and coverage begins the following January. Check with your plan, though. Some plans have stricter enrollment rules than others. And some limit the number of Medicare patients they accept, so they may skip one or more enrollment periods.

To evaluate a plan you're eligible for, you can use the Medicare Health Plan Compare tool on the Medicare website, www.Medicare.gov. It can help you compare costs, coverage, plan quality, and patient satisfaction. Once you've chosen a plan, you request an enrollment card from the plan, and return it before the deadline.

If you decide to drop out of a Medicare+Choice plan, or if the plan ends, you'll be automatically enrolled in original Medicare, so that there's no gap in your coverage. But if you want to join another Medicare+Choice plan, you may have to wait until the following November.

THE TIME TO BUY

The time to buy Medigap insurance is within the first six months of enrolling in Medicare Part B. During that period, insurance companies must sell you the plan you want.

That's particularly important if you have any health problems that put you into a high-risk category, such as being a smoker or overweight.

If you have a pre-existing condition, an insurer can refuse to cover treatment for that ailment for the first six months. But if you miss the initial six-month application period, your application can be rejected.

ISSUE AGE

NO AGE

ATTAINED AGE

B

When you buy your policy, you must also choose a **rating method**, or the way your premiums will be calculated. An **issue age rating** means that your premium is determined by how old you are when you buy and stays the same as long as your policy is in effect. A **no age**, or community **rating**, means that everyone who has the policy pays the same premium, regardless of age. And an **attained age rating** means that your premium goes up as you get older.

Experts recommend that you compare an issue age rating and a no age rating for the most economical long-term coverage. Attained age plans usually cost less in the first five years but are the most expensive in the long run.

HANG ON TO MEDIGAP?

If you switch to a Medicare+Choice plan, you might want to keep your Medigap insurance. It can be hard to get new Medigap coverage if you decide to return to original Medicare. You'll be paying for coverage that you won't be using, but you might decide it's worth the cost until you see how your new plan works out.

Long-term Care

As you get older, you may need help taking care of yourself.

The longer you live, the greater the likelihood that you'll need **long-term care**, sometimes known as elder care or custodial care. Long-term care can be provided at home, in an assisted living center, or in a nursing home.

Unless you're getting hospice care because you're terminally ill, or qualify for **Medicaid**, the state-run health insurance program for people with very limited financial resources, the bills for long-term care are your responsibility.

One solution may be to shift part of this potential financial burden to an insurance company by buying a long-term care insurance policy.

CLOSED DOORS

You can't depend on Medicare, the federal health insurance plan for people 65 and older and disabled people of all ages, to pay the costs of long-term care. Medicare will help pay for up to 100 days in a skilled nursing care facility after you've been hospitalized, but nothing after that. It will also cover part-time or occasional skilled healthcare in your home when it's medically necessary.

The key word in both cases is skilled. Skilled care describes medical procedures that must be handled by licensed professionals. If someone without those credentials can provide the care you need, you don't qualify for Medicare coverage at all.

Conventional health insurance doesn't cover long-term personal or custodial care either. And many policies have **payment caps**, which means that even if you did qualify for long-term skilled care, you would eventually exhaust the maximum your insurer would pay and be left without coverage.

AND AN OPENING

Long-term care insurance, on the other hand, is set up to help pay for the costs of care for people with a chronic but not life-threatening illness, a physical disability, or cognitive impairments such as those experienced by Alzheimer's patients.

Like other forms of insurance, long-term care policies have caps, or maximum benefit amounts. That means no policy will pay for the total cost of care. But having this kind of insurance can reduce, sometimes significantly, the amount you're responsible for paying. Long-term care insurance can also give you more flexibility in where and how you choose to have your care provided.

PLAN DETAILS

When you're considering long-term care insurance, it's important to understand the plan's basic features and how each of them influences the cost of coverage and the benefits you'll be entitled to.

A policy will pay a **daily benefit**, or coverage amount, either directly to you or to the care provider for each day you receive care. You choose the amount from a limited set of alternatives, such as $80, $100, or $120 a day.

Each policy also has a specific **benefit period**, which is the length of time, such as two, three, or five years, that the plan will provide coverage.

Each policy has an **elimination period**, or gap between when you begin to incur costs and when the policy begins to pay your daily benefit. You might choose 30, 90, or 180 days.

The larger the daily benefit, the longer the benefit period, and the shorter the elimination period, the more your policy will cost. So you have to balance what you might need against what you're willing or able to pay.

Once you've determined your daily benefit and your benefit period, you can also calculate your maximum benefit amount. You simply multiply the daily benefit by the benefit period. For example, if your policy will pay $80 a day for two years, or 730 days, your maximum benefit is $58,400 ($80 x 730 = $58,400).

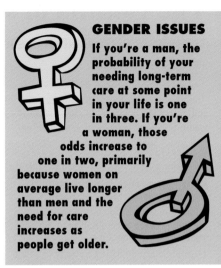

GENDER ISSUES

If you're a man, the probability of your needing long-term care at some point in your life is one in three. If you're a woman, those odds increase to one in two, primarily because women on average live longer than men and the need for care increases as people get older.

INFLATION PROTECTION

One of the most troublesome unknowns in healthcare is what it will cost tomorrow, next year, and 20 years from now. At certain times, healthcare expenses have increased much faster than the rate of inflation, and they've never been lower than they were the year before.

To offset these increases, many long-term care policies let you buy inflation coverage, offering a choice of simple or compounded protection. For example, with simple inflation protection, your daily benefit might increase by 5% of the original amount each year, while with compounded protection, it would increase by 5% of the most recent benefit amount each year.

Other policies let you buy supplemental coverage at some point after your policy takes effect to compensate for increased costs. Although the built-in protection makes a policy more expensive, it's often a better choice.

THE TIME TO BUY

If you decide long-term care insurance makes sense for you, the next question is when to buy. As with other types of insurance, the older you are, the higher the premium you're likely to pay for the same level of coverage. In most cases, you can't buy coverage after you turn 84, though you can continue to be covered by a policy you've purchased earlier.

Experts agree that the best time to buy is between ages 55 and 60. In that case, you can balance a slightly smaller premium against a slightly clearer sense of a suitable daily benefit. The only advantage of waiting until you're 70 is that you don't need the additional cost of inflation protection.

The Details of Coverage

Long-term care insurance sometimes works in mysterious ways.

Just because you have a long-term care policy doesn't mean you'll automatically begin to collect your daily benefit when you begin spending money on custodial healthcare.

All long-term care policies have a list of **trigger events**, sometimes called benefit triggers. They mark the point at which you qualify for your benefit and the elimination period begins. A trigger event might be a doctor's order for custodial care following a stroke or other medical condition. But it is frequently the harder-to-pinpoint time at which you're unable to perform two of the customary six **activities of daily living (ADL)** on your own. Those are bathing, dressing, eating, taking medica-tion, toileting (which means going to the bathroom), and transferring (which means being able to change from a sitting to standing position).

What's more, a trigger event that satisfies the level of need required for home care coverage may not satisfy the requirement for nursing home coverage. Be sure you understand how they differ in your policy, if they do.

DON'T TAKE A BATH ON THIS ONE

Bathing is the first ADL that most people struggle with. If you're considering a policy that lists five ADLs, and bathing isn't one of them, you probably want to look further.

IF YOU CAN'T DO TWO OF THESE ADLs

WHEN IT'S NOT A MEDICAL ISSUE

If you're considering a long-term care policy, you'll want to be sure that it has a benefit trigger for cognitive impair-ment. That's the formal way of describing the effects of Alzheimer's and related diseases that affect your ability to live independently.

More people who need long-term care need it for cognitive impairment than for any other reason. But if you're able to manage the normal activities of daily living, you won't qualify for coverage without the added cognitive trigger.

Remember, though, that once you have been diagnosed with Alzheimer's, you probably won't be able to buy cover-age for that condition.

OPTIONAL COVERAGE

The premium you pay for long-term care insurance is determined primarily by the daily benefit and benefit period you choose, your age when you buy the policy, how healthy you are, and the company that issues the policy.

But you can usually add optional benefits, which while they increase the cost of your insurance, provide some potentially important protections.

A **nonforfeiture clause** guarantees that you'll get a portion of your premiums back if you let the policy lapse, or if you die while the policy is in force.

A **waiver of premium** lets you stop paying your premium during the period that you're getting benefits without putting your coverage in jeopardy. Your policy may limit the number of months that the waiver will apply.

A PLAN WISH LIST

According to the **National Association of Insurance Commissioners (NAIC)**, there are some features you should be sure are included in any long-term care policy you buy:

- Coverage for Alzheimer's disease
- No requirement that you have to be hospitalized as a precondition of qualifying for benefits
- No requirement that you must receive skilled nursing care before qualifying for custodial care coverage
- An inflation protection option
- No requirement that you spend time in a nursing home before qualifying for home care
- A guaranteed renewable clause that ensures your policy can't be revoked or canceled as you age or if you're ill
- At least a one-year benefit period for nursing home or at-home care

You also want to be sure that any pre-existing condition exclusion is no longer than six months.

As far as cost goes, group policies you may have access to through your employer will probably be cheaper than coverage you can buy on your own. They may also be more likely to offer the nonforfeiture option and a waiver of premium. But you'll still want to check out what might be available from a professional association or other group you belong to.

YOU MAY QUALIFY FOR HOME CARE

A MATTER OF NUMBERS

You can deduct the cost of your annual long-term care premiums if they, combined with your other out-of-pocket medical expenses, add up to more than 7.5% of your adjusted gross income. But experts caution that you shouldn't be spending more than 5% to 7% of your income to buy this type of protection.

TRY SELF-INSURANCE

You can create your own long-term insurance plan by opening one or more investment accounts or buying an annuity to provide the income you'd need to pay for long-term care. That's known as self-insurance.

If you start investing the money you'd otherwise pay in premiums early enough, you may be able to build a significant protective cushion that you could use as you chose if it turned out you never needed long-term care. But adequate self-insurance depends on the amount you invest, the investment choices you make, and the state of the economy.

Some experts suggest that self-insurance is a good idea only for people who have more than $1 million in investable assets, not counting their real estate holdings.

GOVERNMENT PROTECTION

Residents of some states—including California, Connecticut, New York, Indiana, Illinois, and Washington—can take advantage of a partnership program that helps protect your financial assets. If you buy long-term care insurance through a partnership and use up your coverage, you may be eligible for Medicaid before you've completely drained your savings.

INDEX

INDEX